Great Escapes
North America

Photos by Don Freeman   *Texts by* Daisann McLane   *Edited by* Angelika Taschen

Great Escapes
North America

TASCHEN

HONG KONG KÖLN LONDON LOS ANGELES MADRID PARIS TOKYO

Emerald Lake Lodge, *Field, British Columbia* 008 ●

Amangani, *Jackson Hole* 344 ●

Calistoga Ranch, *Calistoga* 292 ●
Auberge du Soleil, *Rutherford* 282 ●
Wilbur Hot Springs, *Wilbur Springs* 272 ●
The Carneros Inn, *Napa* 264 ●

Sundance, *Sundance* 336 ●

Sky Hotel, *Aspen* 328 ●

● 302 The Ahwahnee, *Yosemite National Park*

● 314 Dunton Hot Springs

Deetjen's Big Sur Inn, *Big Sur* 234 ●
Post Ranch Inn, *Big Sur* 242 ●

Madonna Inn, *San Luis Obispo* 252 ●

El Capitan Canyon, *Santa Barbara* 226 ●

Hope Springs Resort, *Desert Hot Springs* 200 ●

Parker Palm Springs, *Palm Springs* 208 ●
Korakia Pensione, *Palm Springs* 218 ●

● 188 Furnace Creek Inn, *Death Valley*

● 134 El Monte Sagrado, *Taos*
140 The Mabel Dodge Luhan House, *Taos*
● 152 Ten Thousand Waves, *Sante Fe*

● 158 Hotel Congress, *Tucson*
166 Rancho de la Osa, *Tucson*

Shady Dell RV Park, *Bisbee* 178 ●

● 110 The Hotel Paisano, *Marfa*
116 Thunderbird Motel, *Marfa*
124 Cibolo Creek Ranch, *Marfa*

Hotel San José, *Austin* 100 ●

"This land is your land, this land is my land, from California to the New York island"
from Woody Guthrie's famous song "This land is your land"

"Head out on the highway, looking for adventure and whatever comes our way"
from the Steppenwolf rock song "Born to be Wild"

Dolores

● 036 The Seth Peterson Cottage, *Lake Delton*

Langdon Hall, *Cambridge, Ontario* 020 ●

Trout Point Lodge, *Kemptville, Nova Scotia* 026 ●

● 042 The Point, *Saranac Lake*

● 050 Wheatleigh, *Lenox*

● 058 Land's End Inn, *Provincetown*

● 070 The Wauwinet, *Nantucket*

● 078 The Moorings Village, *Islamorada*

● 088 Little Palm Island, *Little Torch Key*

Contents   Inhalt   Sommaire

Price categories:
$ up to 150 US$
$$ up to 250 US$
$$$ up to 450 US$
$$$$ over 450 US$

Preiskategorien:
$ bis 150 US$
$$ bis 250 US$
$$$ bis 450 US$
$$$$ über 450 US$

Catégories de prix:
$ jusqu'à 150 US$
$$ jusqu'à 250 US$
$$$ jusqu'à 450 US$
$$$$ plus de 450 US$

Canadian Jewel...
Emerald Lake Lodge, Field, British Columbia

Emerald Lake Lodge, Field, British Columbia

Canadian Jewel

Sometimes nature startles us with a display of color that seems almost unreal, too stunning not to be a mirage or digitally enhanced. But the intense, opaque aquamarine green of Emerald Lake, high in the Canadian Rockies, is real, just as real now as it was in the late 19th century, when the Canadian Railroad company's workers were pushing the rails westward through this challenging mountain terrain. The Canadian Railroad company built grand hotels and lodges along the rail lines, to lure tourists out to the wilds of western Canada. Nearly 100 years later, these marvellous buildings, great examples of Canadian vernacular architecture, still continue to welcome visitors to Canada's wilderness. Emerald Lake Lodge is one of the more remote of the railroad lodges; until it was restored and expanded in the 1980s, it was just a couple of cabins by the lake surrounded by white-capped mountains. The eco-sensitive renovation and expansion has not disturbed the impressive isolation and beauty of the area–visitors must leave their cars a distance away, and take a shuttle bus to the lodge. Inside your log cottage room, a warm stone fireplace awaits; ski trails and hiking trails begin right outside your door. But after hiking to high mountain meadows thick with wildflowers, you can return to civilization (and to dinner in the lodge's fine restaurant). Step out onto the wooden porch, relax in a cushioned chair under a blanket, snug against the chill, and take a deep breath of this crisp, clean Canadian air. The lake spreads before you, reflecting mountains and fir trees in splendid stillness.

Book to Pack: "Call of the Wild" by Jack London.
Famous novel about life in the far north woods.

Emerald Lake Lodge		
P.O. Box 10		
Field, British Columbia V0A 1G0		
Canada		
Tel. +1 250 343 6321		
Fax +1 250 343 6724		
Email: ellmanager@crmr.com		
Website: www.crmr.com		
www.great-escapes-hotels.com		

DIRECTIONS	In Yoho National Park, 25 miles (40 km) west of Lake Louise; about 125 miles (200 km) west of Calgary airport.	
RATES	$$	
ROOMS	100 rooms in 24 log chalets.	
FOOD	Fine dining (California and "mountain" cuisine with local wild game) in Mount Burgess Dining Room; casual meals in Kicking Horse Lounge.	
HISTORY	Originally built by the Canadian Pacific Railroad in 1902; renovated and expanded in 1986.	
X-FACTOR	A cozy stay in the most breathtaking natural setting in Canada.	

Ein bisschen Frieden

Die Natur stellt sich manchmal kitschiger dar als ein digital bearbeitetes Farbfoto. So als würde man in einem Werbeprospekt blättern oder unter heftigen Sinnestäuschungen leiden. Wie etwa beim Anblick des milchig-aquamarinen Grüns des »Emerald Lake« in den kanadischen Rocky Mountains. Der auffällige See wurde im späten 19. Jahrhundert von Bahnarbeitern entdeckt, als sie sich während des Baus einer Bahnlinie über die Rockies abrackerten. Um Touristen in die unberührte Natur des Westens zu locken, ließ die kanadische Eisenbahngesellschaft entlang dieser Bahnlinien Grand Hotels und Lodges bauen. Fast hundert Jahre später kommen immer noch Touristen in die wunderschöne Landschaft und übernachten in den Hotels beispielhafter kanadischer Alltagsarchitektur. »Emerald Lake Lodge« ist eine dieser Eisenbahn-Lodges und wohl am weitesten von der Zivilisation entfernt. Ein paar Hütten vor schneebedeckten Bergen waren bis zur öko-verträglichen Renovierung in den Achtzigern alles, was hier stand. Diese brachte zwar mehr Komfort, änderte aber nichts an der Unberührtheit, Stille und Schönheit der umliegenden Natur. Die Anlage ist autofrei – die Gäste lassen ihre Autos ein Stück weiter draußen auf einem Parkplatz und werden per Shuttle-Bus zur Lodge gefahren. In den Zimmern der Blockhütten flämmelt ein wärmendes Feuer im Steinkamin, Ski- und Wanderwege führen direkt bis vor die Haustür. Nach einer ausgiebigen Wanderung durch die mit Wildblumen übersäten Bergwiesen kann man sich auf der Holzveranda bei kristallklarer Luft, eingekuschelt in Decken und Kissen, schön entspannen.

Buchtipp: »Der Ruf der Wildnis« von Jack London.
Berühmter Roman über das Leben in den Wäldern von Alaska.

Joyau du Canada

Parfois la nature nous coupe le souffle avec ses couleurs presque surnaturelles, si incroyables qu'on croirait un mirage ou une photo retouchée. Mais le bleu-vert opaque d' « Emerald Lake », haut perché dans les Rocheuses canadiennes, est tout aussi réel aujourd'hui qu'à la fin du 19e siècle, quand les ouvriers de la compagnie des chemins de fer progressaient péniblement vers l'Ouest, posant les rails dans les montagnes. La compagnie construisit de grands hôtels et des gîtes le long de la voie pour attirer les touristes. Près de 100 ans plus tard, ces merveilleux bâtiments, belles illustrations de l'architecture canadienne, continuent d'accueillir les visiteurs en pleine nature. Jusqu'à ce qu'elle soit restaurée et agrandie dans les années quatre-vingt, « Emerald Lake Lodge » ne comptait que quelques cabanes au bord du lac ceint de sommets enneigés. Les modifications respectueuses de l'environnement n'ont pas détruit l'isolement et la beauté du lieu. Les visiteurs doivent laisser leurs voitures à une certaine distance et emprunter une navette. À l'intérieur de votre cabane en bois, une cheminée en pierre vous attend. Les pistes de ski et les sentiers de randonnée démarrent sur le pas de votre porte. Après une ballade dans les prés montagneux envahis de fleurs sauvages, vous retrouverez la civilisation (et un bon dîner) dans l'excellent restaurant de la lodge. Détendez-vous sous une couverture dans un fauteuil douillet ou sortez sur votre porche en bois pour inspirer un grand bol de l'air pur du Canada. Le lac s'étend à vos pieds, reflétant les massifs et les pins dans un calme splendide.

Livre à emporter : « L'Appel de la forêt » de Jack London.
Célèbre roman sur la vie dans les forêts du Grand Nord.

ANREISE	Im Yoho National Park, 40 km westlich von Lake Louise; rund 200 km westlich vom Flughafen Calgary.
PREISE	$$
ZIMMER	100 Zimmer in 24 Chalets.
KÜCHE	Elegante kalifornische Küche im »Mount Burgess Dining Room«, auf der Karte stehen auch Wild-Gerichte; einfache Menüs in der »Kicking Horse Lounge«.
GESCHICHTE	1902 von der Canadian Pacific Railroad gebaut, 1986 renoviert und erweitert.
X-FAKTOR	Gemütliche Unterkunft in atemberaubend schöner Naturlandschaft im Westen Kanadas.

ACCÈS	Dans le parc national Yoho, à 40 km à l'ouest de Lake Louise; environ 200 km à l'ouest de l'aéroport de Calgary.
PRIX	$$
CHAMBRES	100 chambres dans 24 chalets.
RESTAURATION	Menus gastronomiques dans la « Mount Burgess Dining Room » ; repas plus simples dans la « Kicking Horse Lounge ».
HISTOIRE	Construit par le Canadian Pacific Railroad en 1902 ; rénové et agrandi en 1986.
LE « PETIT PLUS »	Un séjour douillet dans le décor naturel le plus époustouflant du Canada.

Timeless Country Life...
Langdon Hall, Cambridge, Ontario

Langdon Hall, Cambridge, Ontario

Timeless Country Life

The English country life used to be the exclusive province of the old moneyed and titled classes, but nowadays it seems like every other rock star and newly-minted dot-com zillionaire owns a grand estate with stables, gardens, and valets, the better to play lord or lady of the manor. The good news is that not all the gorgeous English country houses belong to Elton John and Madonna. About an hour's drive outside of Toronto is a 200 acre estate that's a near-perfect replica of an English country manse. Langdon Hall is an elegant, columned Federal revival mansion that was built in the 19th century as a summer home for the granddaughter of New York mogul John Jacob Astor. Like many such houses, it was so huge that when the great fortunes dissipated, the property became too expensive to maintain privately. Eventually Langdon Hall was converted to a hotel, and today it is a place where one can enjoy the British country life for a few days. The highlight of this Relais & Châteaux inn is its magnificent English garden, with four trails for strolling through flower beds or woods, and a lawn for playing, yes, croquet. Some contemporary touches, like a heated swimming pool, and a full-service spa, are balanced by some very old-school ones, like a traditional afternoon tea served in the conservatory. The rooms, with big beds, overstuffed chairs, and de luxe European-style bathrooms, have natural gas radiant heating under the hardwood floors, a touch of creature comfort as understated and luxurious as everything else in this picture perfect manor.

Book to Pack: "Pride and Prejudice" by Jane Austen.
Lives and loves of the landed gentry in the beginning of the 19th century - very often filmed.

Langdon Hall
1 Langdon Drive
Cambridge, Ontario N3H 4R8
Canada
Tel. +1 519 740 2100
Fax +1 519 740 8161
Email : reservations@langdonhall.ca
Website: www.langdonhall.ca
www.great-escapes-hotels.com

DIRECTIONS	45 miles (70 km) west of Toronto Airport.
RATES	$$$
ROOMS	53 guest rooms and suites.
FOOD	Dining room on premises; fine cuisine and regional dishes, indoor and outdoor dining. Continental breakfast.
HISTORY	Originally built in 1898 as a summer home for the granddaughter of U.S. millionare John Jacob Astor; renovated in 1987 as an inn.
X-FACTOR	A timelessly grand country estate, complete with croquet lawn.

Leben wie der Landadel

Das englische Landleben war lange ein Privileg des Geld- und sonstigen Adels. Heutzutage spielen nun aber auch gewöhnliche Rockstars und Dot-Com-Multimillionäre Lord oder Lady auf Landgütern mit Pferdeställen, Gartenanlagen und Dienern. Doch zum Glück gehören nicht alle dieser prächtigen Herrenhäuser einer Madonna oder einem Elton John. Ungefähr eine Autostunde außerhalb von Toronto in Kanada befindet sich auf einem 80 Hektar großen Grundstück eine originalgetreue Replika eines englischen Landgutes. Das mit Säulen verzierte elegante Herrenhaus »Langdon Hall« wurde im 19. Jahrhundert für die Enkelin des New Yorker Tycoons John Jacob Astor gebaut. Es ist wie die meisten solcher Gutsbesitze riesig, und als mit der Zeit das Familienvermögen zerrann, wurde der Unterhalt für die Familie zu kostspielig. Schließlich wurde »Langdon Hall« zu einem Hotel umfunktioniert, und die Gäste können hier für ein paar Tage den Lifestyle des britischen Landadels genießen. Das Schönste an diesem »Relais-&-Châteaux«-Hotel ist die englische Gartenanlage mit vier Pfaden, die durch Blumenbeete und Wälder führen. Dazu gehört ein Rasen, auf dem Krocket gespielt wird. Mit dem Umbau wurden ein paar Konzessionen an heutige Zeiten gemacht: Ein geheizter Swimming-Pool und ein Full-Service-Spa gehören dazu. Das Haus hält allerdings an seinen Traditionen fest. So wird ein Afternoon-Tea im Konservatorium serviert. Die Zimmer sind mit großen Betten, gepolsterten Stühlen und luxuriösen Badezimmern mit Bodenheizung ausgestattet. »Langdon Hall« ist ein schönes Beispiel für die Eleganz britischen Understatements.

Buchtipp: »Stolz und Vorurteil« von Jane Austen.
Leben und Lieben des englischen Landadels zu Beginn des 19. Jahrhunderts – mehrfach verfilmt.

La grande vie à la campagne

La campagne anglaise était autrefois l'apanage des vieilles familles fortunées et de l'aristocratie mais, de nos jours, il semblerait que toute rock star et nouveau super riche point-com se doivent de posséder son grand domaine avec écuries, parc et valets afin de mieux jouer au châtelain et à la châtelaine. Bonne nouvelle : toutes les somptueuses gentilhommières n'appartiennent pas à Elton John ou à Madonna. À une heure de route de Toronto, sur une propriété de 80 hectares, l'élégant « Langdon Hall », réplique d'un presbytère anglais revu et corrigé dans le style nordiste du 18e siècle, vous accueille sous son porche à colonnade. Le magnat new-yorkais John Jacob Astor le fit construire au 19e siècle comme résidence d'été pour sa petite-fille. Comme beaucoup de ces demeures immenses, une fois la fortune dilapidée, elle devint trop lourde à entretenir. Convertie en hôtel, on peut aujourd'hui y goûter aux joies distinguées de la campagne l'espace de quelques jours. Le joyau de ce bastion des « Relais & Châteaux » est le parc, avec son magnifique jardin à l'anglaise, son bois et sa pelouse où l'on joue, of course, au croquet. Les touches contemporaines telles que la piscine chauffée en plein air et le spa sophistiqué sont contrebalancées par les rituels traditionnels tel le thé de cinq heures servi dans le jardin d'hiver. Les chambres, équipées de grands lits, de profonds fauteuils et de belles salles de bain à l'européenne, sont chauffées au gaz naturel par le plancher, un détail aussi discret et luxueux que tout le reste dans ce manoir de carte postale.

Livre à emporter : « Orgueil et préjugés » de Jane Austen.
La vie et les amours de l'aristocratie anglaise au début du 19e siècle – plusieurs fois adapté au cinéma.

ANREISE	70 km westlich vom Flughafen Toronto.	
PREISE	$$$	
ZIMMER	53 Gästezimmer und Suiten.	
KÜCHE	Speisesaal mit Terrasse; elegante Küche, regionale Gerichte. Kontinentales Frühstück.	
GESCHICHTE	1898 als Sommerresidenz für die Enkelin von US-Millionär John Jacob Astor erbaut; 1987 renoviert und als Hotel eröffnet.	
X-FAKTOR	Prächtiges klassisches Landgut mit einer Krocket-Rasenanlage.	

ACCÈS	À 70 km à l'ouest de l'aéroport de Toronto.
PRIX	$$$
CHAMBRES	53 chambres et suites.
RESTAURATION	Cuisine gastronomique et plats régionaux, servis dans la salle à manger ou en terrasse. Petit-déjeuner continental.
HISTOIRE	Construit en 1898 comme résidence d'été pour la petite-fille du millionnaire américain John Jacob Astor ; rénové en 1987 et converti en hôtel.
LE « PETIT PLUS »	L'atmosphère atemporelle d'une grande demeure de campagne, parfaite jusque dans sa pelouse de croquet.

Cajun Roots...
Trout Point Lodge, Kemptville, Nova Scotia

Trout Point Lodge, Kemptville, Nova Scotia

Cajun Roots

A bitter history links the Canadian island of Nova Scotia with the state of Louisiana, far to the south: in 1755, the French settlers in the northeastern part of Canada were forcibly expelled by the British army, and they had to flee south to Louisiana which was then a French colony. The expulsion – called "le grand dérangement"– uprooted thousands of people, and nearly erased the French Acadian culture from the Nova Scotia area. Nearly 250 years later, three successful restauranteurs and gourmets from New Orleans travelled to Nova Scotia in search of their French Acadian ("Cajun") roots. They found roots, and more. The trip through Nova Scotia's fishing villages inspired a best selling cookbook, and it also inspired the trio to open a lodge, cooking school, and gourmet restaurant in the backwoods of Nova Scotia. Trout Point Lodge is somewhat like an overgrown cabin, made of local wood, with a long second story porch; the beds, chairs and tables are handmade from saplings. Here you can learn to cook a courtbouillon with seafood recently plucked from the ocean, or go fishing or hiking. Or, you can just hang out and relax on the porch with a glass of fine French wine, and celebrate the triumphant Canadian return of these food-loving Louisiana Cajuns.

Book to Pack: "Evangeline" by Henry Wadsworth Longfellow. Classic American poem about the migration of the French Acadian settlers from Nova Scotia to New Orleans.

Trout Point Lodge
189 Trout Point Road off the East Branch Road
East Kemptville, Yarmouth County, Nova Scotia
B0W 1Y0
Canada
Tel. +1 902 482 8360
Email: info@canticumhotels.com;
troutpoint@foodvacation.com
Website: www.troutpoint.com
www.great-escapes-hotels.com

DIRECTIONS	23 miles (37 km) northeast of Yarmouth, Nova Scotia.
RATES	$
ROOMS	13 rooms and suites, a two bedroom cottage, and a 12 bed lodge.
FOOD	The Dining Room restaurant serves Creole and Cajun inspired gourmet dishes, emphasis on fresh seafood; cooking seminars are also regularly held at Trout Point.
HISTORY	Founded by three cookbook authors from New Orleans.
X-FACTOR	Explore the roots of French New World (Cajun and Creole) cuisine in a rustic woodsy retreat.

Zurück zu den Wurzeln

Die kanadische Insel Nova Scotia und der US-Staat Louisiana verbindet ein unrühmliches Stück Geschichte. Nachdem
die französische Krone 1755 ihre kanadischen Besitzungen
an die Briten abtreten mussten, wurden die französischen
Siedler unverzüglich von der Armee des Landes verwiesen.
Die heimatlos gewordenen Menschen flohen Richtung
Süden nach Louisiana, damals noch unter französischer
Herrschaft. Der Landesverweis, »le grand dérangement«
genannt, entwurzelte tausende von Menschen und löschte
die französische Kultur in Nova Scotia beinahe ganz aus.
Rund 250 Jahre später machten sich drei erfolgreiche fran-
zösischstämmige Gastronome und Feinschmecker aus New
Orleans, Louisiana, auf die Suche nach ihren Wurzeln in
Nova Scotia. Die Reise durch die Fischerdörfer von Nova
Scotia inspirierte das Trio zu einem Kochbuch über kreoli-
sche Küche und ihre französischen Ursprünge, das schnell
zu einem Bestseller wurde. Der nächste Schritt war nahelie-
gend: Die erfolgreichen Kochbuchautoren eröffneten im
Hinterland von Nova Scotia eine Gäste-Lodge mt einem
Gourmetrestaurant und einer Kochschule. »Trout Point
Lodge« ist eine gemütliche Blockhütte mit zweistöckiger
Veranda, umgeben von einem Pflanzendschungel. Die
Betten, Stühle und Tische sind alle aus jungen Zweigen
handgefertigt. Mitten im Grünen kann man hier etwas über
die Ursprünge der Cajun-Küche erfahren und dabei lernen,
wie man eine Court Bouillon mit Fischen und Meeres-
früchten zubereitet.

Buchtipp: »Evangeline« von Henry Wadsworth Longfellow.
Klassisch amerikanisches Gedicht über französische Siedler,
die Nova Scotia verließen, um nach New Orleans auszuwan-
dern.

Racines acadiennes

Une histoire cruelle lie l'île de Nouvelle-Écosse à l'état de la
Louisiane : en 1755, les colons français du nord-est canadien
furent expulsés manu militari par l'armé britannique et se
réfugièrent tout au sud, parmi leurs compatriotes de Louisiane. Ce « grand dérangement » déracina des milliers de
personnes et faillit anéantir la culture acadienne la Nouvelle-
Écosse. Près de 250 ans plus tard, trois restaurateurs de
talent et fins gourmets de la Nouvelle-Orléans firent le périple inverse à la recherche de leurs racines. Ils y trouvèrent
bien plus que cela : les villages de leurs ancêtres leur inspi-
rèrent un livre de recettes qui fit un tabac et les convainqui-
rent d'ouvrir un gîte, une école de cuisine et un restaurant
gastronomique dans l'arrière-pays de l'île. Construite en rondins de bois, « Trout Point Lodge » ressemble à une cabane
démesurée avec son long porche à l'étage. Les chaises, les
lits et les tables artisanales ont été réalisés dans de jeunes
arbres locaux. Ici, on peut apprendre à préparer un courtbouillon avec des fruits de mer frais du jour même, aller à la
pêche ou en randonnée. À moins qu'on préfère se détendre
sur le porche avec un verre de bon vin français et célébrer le
retour triomphal au Canada de ces trois Cajuns de Louisiane
amateurs de bonne chère.

**Livre à emporter : « Evangeline » d'Henry Wadsworth
Longfellow.**
Classique de la poésie américaine sur l'exode des colons aca-
diens de la Nouvelle-Écosse à la Nouvelle-Orléans.

ANREISE	37 km nordöstlich von Yarmouth, Nova Scotia.	ACCÈS	À 37 km au nord-est de Yarmouth, en Nouvelle-Ècosse.
PREISE	$	PRIX	$
ZIMMER	13 Zimmer und Suiten, ein Cottage mit zwei Schlafzim- mern, eine Lodge mit 12 Betten.	CHAMBRES	13 chambres et suites, un cottage avec deux chambres à coucher et une cabane de 12 lits.
KÜCHE	Im Restaurant »Dining Room« gibt's kreolische Küche und Cajun-Food – auf der Menükarte stehen viele Fischgerichte; in der »Trout Point Lodge« werden zudem Kochkurse durchgeführt.	RESTAURANT	Le « Dining Room » sert une cuisine gastronomique d'inspiration créole et cajun. Des séminaires de cuisine sont régulièrement organisés.
GESCHICHTE	Von drei Kochbuchautoren aus New Orleans eröffnet.	HISTOIRE	Fondé par les trois auteurs d'un livre de cuisine origi- naires de la Nouvelle-Orléans.
X-FAKTOR	Kreolisches Essen und Cajun-Food in rustikaler Umgebung.	LE « PETIT PLUS »	Explorez les racines de la cuisine française du nouveau monde dans une retraite au fond des bois.

The Wright Stuff...
The Seth Peterson Cottage, Lake Delton

The Seth Peterson Cottage, Lake Delton

The Wright Stuff

It is a rare and special thing to be able to spend a vacation retreat inside a work of art. The Seth Peterson Cottage was one of Frank Lloyd Wright's last commissions as an architect, in 1958, and today it is the only one of his houses available for rental by the general public. Staying here is a total immersion in his revolutionary design principles – the house has been described as "having more architecture per square foot than any other building he ever designed." From outside the cottage is a beautifully realized structure made of wood and natural sandstone that harmonizes with the wooded terrain of the remote Wisconsin state park where it is located. Light floods inside through floor to ceiling windows that embody Wright's principle of blending the exterior and interior. Inside, Wright's trademark massive stone fireplace is the center of an open living space that is furnished with custom-built furniture. The vacation cottage, designed for a local businessman who died before it was completed, had languished and fallen into disrepair until it was rediscovered by a community activist. Together with a group of citizens concerned about preservation, she formed a non-profit trust to renovate the cottage strictly according to Wright's original vision. At the Seth Peterson Cottage Wright's ideas come alive for the lucky guests who can spend a lazy weekend here, sitting on Wright-designed chairs, gazing through his wall of glass at the beautiful woods beyond.

Book to Pack: "An Autobiography" by Frank Lloyd Wright.
Written by the master architect of the 20th century while in seclusion in a cabin in Minnesota.

The Seth Peterson Cottage
Sand County Service Company
Box 409
Lake Delton, WI 53940
Tel. +1 608 254 6551
Fax +1 608 254 4400
Email: sandcnty@midplains.net
Website: www.sethpeterson.org
www.great-escapes-hotels.com

DIRECTIONS	About 50 miles (80 km) northwest of Madison, Wisconsin.
RATES	$$
ROOMS	The cottage holds up to 4 overnight guests.
FOOD	Self-catering.
HISTORY	Designed by Wright for Wisconsin native Seth Peterson in 1958; restored in 1992.
X-FACTOR	The only Frank Lloyd Wright house available for rental to the general public.

Architekturlegende

Ganz, ganz selten ist es möglich, in einem Kunstwerk zu leben. Eine der großen Ausnahmen ist das »Seth Peterson Cottage« – das letzte Auftragswerk von Frank Lloyd Wright aus dem Jahr 1958. Das Cottage kann man heute mieten und damit die revolutionären Architektur-Prinzipien Wrights hautnah erleben. Bewunderer des Baus meinen, in keinem anderen Werk Wrights gäbe es so viel Architektur wie in diesem. Das Cottage aus Holz und Sandstein schmiegt sich in die bewaldete Umgebung des Wisconsin State Park perfekt ein. Riesige Panoramafenster lassen reichlich Licht ins Innere und verkörpern so Wrights Grundsatz, die Grenzen zwischen Innen und Außen aufzulösen. In der Mitte des offenen Wohnraums mit maßgefertigten Möbeln steht, typisch für Wright, ein massiver Steinkamin. Wright erhielt den Auftrag für den Bau des Feriencottages vom Geschäftsmann Seth Peterson. Doch noch bevor der Bau fertig gestellt war, segnete dieser das Zeitliche, und lange kümmerte sich niemand darum. Ein Bewohner der Gemeinde entdeckte dann das halb zerfallene Werk des legendären Architekten und tat sich mit einer Gruppe von Leuten zusammen, die sich für die Erhaltung bedeutender Bauwerke einsetzt. Zusammen gründeten sie einen Non-Profit-Fonds. Mit diesem Geld wurde das Cottage ganz genau nach den Vorstellungen Wrights in Stand gesetzt und die Ideen des Architekten damit zu neuem Leben erweckt.

Buchtipp: »Frank Lloyd Wright« von Bruce Brooks Pfeiffer.
Ein Überblick über die Werke des bedeutenden amerikanischen Architekten.

Vivre dans l'art

On n'a pas tous les jours l'occasion de passer ses vacances dans une œuvre d'art. Le « Seth Peterson Cottage », dernière commande de Frank Lloyd Wright en 1958, est aujourd'hui sa seule demeure que l'on peut louer. Y séjourner constitue une immersion complète dans ses principes architecturaux révolutionnaires. La maison a été décrite comme « possédant plus d'architecture au mètre carré que n'importe quelle autre de ses créations ». De dehors, c'est une superbe structure en bois et en grès naturel qui s'harmonise avec le paysage boisé du parc de l'état du Wisconsin. La lumière inonde les pièces grâce aux baies vitrées, Wright ayant toujours cherché à fondre l'intérieur et l'extérieur. L'espace de séjour ouvert est dominé par une cheminée centrale massive et aménagé de meubles sur-mesure. Cette ancienne résidence d'été, construite pour un homme d'affaires de la région mort avant son achèvement, tombait en ruines quand elle a été redécouverte par la militante d'une association locale. Avec d'autres citoyens soucieux du patrimoine, ils ont créé un trust à but non lucratif pour la restaurer conformément à la vision originale de l'architecte. Au « Seth Peterson Cottage », les idées de Wright prennent vie pour les heureux élus qui y passent un week-end paresseux, assis dans les fauteuils qu'il a dessinés, contemplant la belle forêt environnante à travers son mur de verre.

Livre à emporter : « Autobiographie » de Frank Lloyd Wright.
Écrite par le maître architecte du 20e siècle alors qu'il était reclus dans une cabane du Minnesota.

ANREISE	Etwa 80 km nordwestlich von Madison, Wisconsin.
PREISE	$$
ZIMMER	Im Cottage können bis zu vier Personen übernachten.
KÜCHE	Für das Essen muss man selber sorgen.
GESCHICHTE	Von Architekturlegende Frank Lloyd Wright im Auftrag von Seth Peterson 1958 entworfen; 1992 restauriert.
X-FAKTOR	Das einzige Haus von Frank Lloyd Wright, das man mieten kann.

Accès	À environ 80 km au nord-ouest de Madison, dans le Wisconsin.
Prix	$$
Chambres	Le cottage peut loger 4 personnes à la fois.
Restauration	Cuisine équipée pour préparer ses repas.
Histoire	Conçu par Wright pour un natif du Wisconsin, Seth Peterson, en 1958 ; restauré en 1992.
Le « petit plus »	La seule maison de Frank Lloyd Wright que le grand public peut louer.

The Wright Stuff

It is a rare and special thing to be able to spend a vacation retreat inside a work of art. The Seth Peterson Cottage was one of Frank Lloyd Wright's last commissions as an architect, in 1958, and today it is the only one of his houses available for rental by the general public. Staying here is a total immersion in his revolutionary design principles – the house has been described as "having more architecture per square foot than any other building he ever designed." From outside the cottage is a beautifully realized structure made of wood and natural sandstone that harmonizes with the wooded terrain of the remote Wisconsin state park where it is located. Light floods inside through floor to ceiling windows that embody Wright's principle of blending the exterior and interior. Inside, Wright's trademark massive stone fireplace is the center of an open living space that is furnished with custom-built furniture. The vacation cottage, designed for a local businessman who died before it was completed, had languished and fallen into disrepair until it was rediscovered by a community activist. Together with a group of citizens concerned about preservation, she formed a non-profit trust to renovate the cottage strictly according to Wright's original vision. At the Seth Peterson Cottage Wright's ideas come alive for the lucky guests who can spend a lazy weekend here, sitting on Wright-designed chairs, gazing through his wall of glass at the beautiful woods beyond.

Book to Pack: "An Autobiography" by Frank Lloyd Wright.
Written by the master architect of the 20th century while in seclusion in a cabin in Minnesota.

The Seth Peterson Cottage
Sand County Service Company
Box 409
Lake Delton, WI 53940
Tel. +1 608 254 6551
Fax +1 608 254 4400
Email: sandcnty@midplains.net
Website: www.sethpeterson.org
www.great-escapes-hotels.com

DIRECTIONS	About 50 miles (80 km) northwest of Madison, Wisconsin.
RATES	$$
ROOMS	The cottage holds up to 4 overnight guests.
FOOD	Self-catering.
HISTORY	Designed by Wright for Wisconsin native Seth Peterson in 1958; restored in 1992.
X-FACTOR	The only Frank Lloyd Wright house available for rental to the general public.

Architekturlegende

Ganz, ganz selten ist es möglich, in einem Kunstwerk zu leben. Eine der großen Ausnahmen ist das »Seth Peterson Cottage« – das letzte Auftragswerk von Frank Lloyd Wright aus dem Jahr 1958. Das Cottage kann man heute mieten und damit die revolutionären Architektur-Prinzipien Wrights hautnah erleben. Bewunderer des Baus meinen, in keinem anderen Werk Wrights gäbe es so viel Architektur wie in diesem. Das Cottage aus Holz und Sandstein schmiegt sich in die bewaldete Umgebung des Wisconsin State Park perfekt ein. Riesige Panoramafenster lassen reichlich Licht ins Innere und verkörpern so Wrights Grundsatz, die Grenzen zwischen Innen und Außen aufzulösen. In der Mitte des offenen Wohnraums mit maßgefertigten Möbeln steht, typisch für Wright, ein massiver Steinkamin. Wright erhielt den Auftrag für den Bau des Feriencottages vom Geschäftsmann Seth Peterson. Doch noch bevor der Bau fertig gestellt war, segnete dieser das Zeitliche, und lange kümmerte sich niemand darum. Ein Bewohner der Gemeinde entdeckte dann das halb zerfallene Werk des legendären Architekten und tat sich mit einer Gruppe von Leuten zusammen, die sich für die Erhaltung bedeutender Bauwerke einsetzt. Zusammen gründeten sie einen Non-Profit-Fonds. Mit diesem Geld wurde das Cottage ganz genau nach den Vorstellungen Wrights in Stand gesetzt und die Ideen des Architekten damit zu neuem Leben erweckt.

Buchtipp: »Frank Lloyd Wright« von Bruce Brooks Pfeiffer. Ein Überblick über die Werke des bedeutenden amerikanischen Architekten.

Vivre dans l'art

On n'a pas tous les jours l'occasion de passer ses vacances dans une œuvre d'art. Le « Seth Peterson Cottage », dernière commande de Frank Lloyd Wright en 1958, est aujourd'hui sa seule demeure que l'on peut louer. Y séjourner constitue une immersion complète dans ses principes architecturaux révolutionnaires. La maison a été décrite comme « possédant plus d'architecture au mètre carré que n'importe quelle autre de ses créations ». De dehors, c'est une superbe structure en bois et en grès naturel qui s'harmonise avec le paysage boisé du parc de l'état du Wisconsin. La lumière inonde les pièces grâce aux baies vitrées, Wright ayant toujours cherché à fondre l'intérieur et l'extérieur. L'espace de séjour ouvert est dominé par une cheminée centrale massive et aménagé de meubles sur-mesure. Cette ancienne résidence d'été, construite pour un homme d'affaires de la région mort avant son achèvement, tombait en ruines quand elle a été redécouverte par la militante d'une association locale. Avec d'autres citoyens soucieux du patrimoine, ils ont créé un trust à but non lucratif pour la restaurer conformément à la vision originale de l'architecte. Au « Seth Peterson Cottage », les idées de Wright prennent vie pour les heureux élus qui y passent un week-end paresseux, assis dans les fauteuils qu'il a dessinés, contemplant la belle forêt environnante à travers son mur de verre.

Livre à emporter : « Autobiographie » de Frank Lloyd Wright. Écrite par le maître architecte du 20e siècle alors qu'il était reclus dans une cabane du Minnesota.

ANREISE	Etwa 80 km nordwestlich von Madison, Wisconsin.
PREISE	$$
ZIMMER	Im Cottage können bis zu vier Personen übernachten.
KÜCHE	Für das Essen muss man selber sorgen.
GESCHICHTE	Von Architekturlegende Frank Lloyd Wright im Auftrag von Seth Peterson 1958 entworfen; 1992 restauriert.
X-FAKTOR	Das einzige Haus von Frank Lloyd Wright, das man mieten kann.

Accès	À environ 80 km au nord-ouest de Madison, dans le Wisconsin.
Prix	$$
Chambres	Le cottage peut loger 4 personnes à la fois.
Restauration	Cuisine équipée pour préparer ses repas.
Histoire	Conçu par Wright pour un natif du Wisconsin, Seth Peterson, en 1958 ; restauré en 1992.
Le « petit plus »	La seule maison de Frank Lloyd Wright que le grand public peut louer.

Five Star Wilderness
The Point, Saranac Lake

Five Star Wilderness

During the Gilded Age in the late 19th century, America became an industrial powerhouse. The economy was open and unregulated, and the rich were richer, relative to the rest of America's population, than they have ever been before or since. The names of the period's wealthiest and most prominent tycoons still resonate in U.S. history: Rockefeller, Morgan, Roosevelt. They built fabulous mansions in New York City, but preferred to spend weekend and summer vacations, in this era before air travel, in the remote Adirondack mountains of New York State.

The Point, located in the middle of the Adirondacks on the serene Saranac Lake, is one of the original "Great Camps" built by the industrial magnates of the era. The "camps" were an architectural fantasy of rustic living – the exteriors were roughhewn log facades, but inside, the appointments were as lush and expansive as a palace. The Point, originally built by William Avery Rockefeller, is a complex of cabin lodges fit for a king. Here, on 75 acres of pristine woodlands, giant stone fireplaces blaze in huge central halls with beamed ceilings. Fox, moose and deer heads line the walls. The rooms – here they're called "quarters"– are small private apartments, replete with fireplaces, Oriental rugs, marbled bathrooms with soaking tubs, and beds made from trunk posts that seem to be growing out of the room. A Relais & Châteaux resort, The Point is renowned for its impeccable high-level service to its guests – everything from breakfast in bed to a champagne lake cruise on a classic 33 foot mahogany launch. Here in the beautiful Adirondack woods, the whisper of pines mingles with the whisper of old money.

Book to pack: "The Rise of Theodore Roosevelt" by Edmund Morris.
The definitive, Pulitzer Prize winning biography of the U.S. president who was the Adirondack's most famous vacationer.

The Point	
P.O. Box 1327	
Saranac Lake, NY 12983	
USA	
Tel. +1 800 255 3530 and +1 518 891 5674	
Fax +1 518 891 1152	
Email: info@thepointresort.com	
Website: www.thepointresort.com	
www.great-escapes-hotels.com	

DIRECTIONS	Located in the Adirondack Mountains about 310 miles (500 km) north of New York City.
RATES	$$$$
ROOMS	10 rooms and one suite.
FOOD	Sumptuous breakfasts, served in your private quarters, or in the resort's Great Hall. Five star lunches and dinners, served in the guests-only restaurant. Wines from the private cellar.
HISTORY	Originally "Camp Wonundra", a lavish "great camp" built by wealthy U.S. industrialist William Avery Rockefeller in the late 1800s.
X-FACTOR	Experience wilderness wrapped in luxury, just like a Gilded-Age New York millionaire.

Luxus in der Wildnis

Im späten 19. Jahrhundert brach in Amerika das Goldene Zeitalter an. Das Land entwickelte sich zu einer Industriemacht, die Möglichkeiten für Unternehmer schienen grenzenlos. Tycoons wie Rockefeller, Morgan und Roosevelt begründeten ihre Dynastien, schrieben amerikanische Geschichte und ließen sich in New York City sagenhafte Herrenhäuser bauen. An den Wochenenden und im Sommer zog es sie jedoch in die Abgeschiedenheit der Adirondack Mountains in New York State – damals auch ohne Flugverkehr schnell zu erreichen.

»The Point« am friedlichen Saranac Lake mitten in den Adirondacks, ist eines der »Great Camps«, wie sie damals von den Großindustriellen nach ihren Vorstellungen vom Landleben gebaut wurden. Von außen einfache Blockhütten, sind sie innen so protzig eingerichtet wie in einem Palast. »The Point«, einst der Landsitz von William Avery Rockefeller, besteht aus einer Ansammlung luxuriöser Holzhütten mitten in 30 Hektar unberührten Waldes. In jeder Unterkunft lodert in einem Steinkamin ein Feuer, rustikale Holzbalken stützen die Decken, und an den Wänden hängen ausgestopfte Fuchs-, Elch- und Hirschköpfe. Die Zimmer mit Kaminen, Orientteppichen, Marmorbadezimmern und Bettpfosten aus riesigen Baumstämmen, sind so groß wie Privat-Apartments. »The Point« gehört zur »Relais-&-Châteaux«-Gruppe und bietet entsprechend perfekten Service. Ob Frühstück im Bett oder Champagner-Fahrt auf dem See in einem der 33 Mahagoni-Boote – in den zauberhaften Wäldern von Adirondack lässt es sich so gut leben wie ein Rockefeller.

Buchtipp: »John D. Rockefeller, die Karriere des Wirtschafts-Titanen« von Ron Chernow.
Biografie über den ersten Milliardär der Geschichte.

Un palais en pleine forêt

À la fin du 19e siècle, l'Amérique connut un âge d'or économique qui fit d'elle une puissance industrielle. Jamais les riches n'avaient été aussi riches. Les plus grandes fortunes de l'époque sont entrées dans l'histoire : Rockefeller, Morgan, Roosevelt. Ces magnats bâtirent de fabuleux hôtels particuliers à Manhattan mais, en ces temps d'avant l'aviation, ils préféraient passer leurs week-ends et leurs étés dans les hauteurs isolées des Adirondacks.

Construit par William Avery Rockefeller sur les rives sereines du lac Saranac, « The Point » est l'un de ces « grands campements » des barons de l'industrie. Sorte de fantasme architectural de la vie rustique, leurs façades en rondins de bois brut cachaient des intérieurs aussi spacieux et pavillons dignes d'un roi. Éparpillés sur une trentaine d'hectares en pleine forêt, tous sont construits autour d'une immense salle centrale avec poutres apparentes et cheminées géantes en pierre. Des têtes de renards, d'élans et de cerfs ornent les murs. Les chambres (on les appelle des « quartiers ») sont de petits appartements privés avec cheminées, tapis persans, salles de bain en marbre, lits taillés dans des troncs qui semblent jaillir des murs. Membre des « Relais & Châteaux », « The Point » est renommé pour la qualité de son service impeccable, depuis ses petits déjeuners à ses croisières sur le lac arrosées au champagne dans une vedette en acajou de dix mètres de long. Ici, dans la splendeur de la forêt des Adirondacks, le murmure des pins se mêle à celui des vieilles fortunes.

Livre à emporter : « John D. Rockefeller » de Ron Chernow.
La biografie du premier milliardaire dans l'histoire.

ANREISE	Liegt in den Adirondack Mountains, zirka 500 km nördlich von New York City.
PREISE	$$$$
ZIMMER	10 Zimmer und eine Suite.
KÜCHE	Reichhaltiges Frühstück in Privatgemächern oder der großen Halle. 5-Sterne-Restaurant für Mittag- und Abendessen, nur für Gäste. Weine aus dem Privatkeller.
GESCHICHTE	Das »Camp Wonundra« wurde im späten 19. Jahrhundert vom amerikanischen Industriellen William Avery Rockefeller gebaut.
X-FAKTOR	Wildnis und Luxus – Leben wie die amerikanischen Tycoons des Goldenen Zeitalters.

ACCÈS	Situé dans les montagnes Adirondacks, à environ 500 km au nord de New York.
PRIX	$$$$
CHAMBRES	10 chambres et une suite.
RESTAURATION	Somptueux petits-déjeuners, servis dans vos quartiers privés ou dans le grand hall du complexe. Déjeuners et dîners cinq étoiles, servis dans le restaurant réservé aux clients de l'hôtel.
HISTOIRE	S'appelait à l'origine « Camp Wonundra »et fut construit par William Avery Rockefeller à la fin du 19e siècle.
LE « PETIT PLUS »	Goûtez à la nature en vous drapant dans le luxe.

The Age of Innocence...
Wheatleigh, Lenox

The Age of Innocence

In America the 1890s were a time when a small group of wealthy moguls controlled an enormous amount of money, money they spent, as nouveau riche do, unabashedly and ostentatiously. Historians refer to this time as the "Gilded Age," and the pre-eminent social chronicler of the period was the famed American novelist from Lenox, Massachusetts and New York City, Edith Wharton. Not far from Wharton's old home in Lenox is Wheatleigh, one of the grand, over-the-top country residences that defined the Gilded Age. It is a sprawling copy of a 16th century Florentine palazzo, built as a "summer cottage" by the son of a railroad mogul as a gift to his daughter, who had made a smart marriage to a Spanish Count. One hundred fifty artisans arrived from Italy to do the carvings and plaster work; the famed American landscape architect Frederick Law Olmstead designed the estate grounds. A multimillion dollar renovation in 2000 transformed Wheatleigh into a private resort, closer in design and feel to the tastes of our contemporary Gilded Age. The faux Italian touches are gone, muted soft colors and Asian fabrics are in, and the restaurant is regionally famous, with an award-winning wine list. Wheatleigh seems tailor-made for lovers and honeymooners, and not surprisingly, it is the setting for many wedding parties. We may not live in the Age of Innocence anymore, but at Wheatleigh we can go there for the weekend.

Book to Pack: "The Age of Innocence" by Edith Wharton.
The definitive chronicle of life among the wealthy during the Gilded Age.

Wheatleigh
Hawthorne Road
Lenox, MA 01240
USA
Tel. +1 413 637 0610
Fax +1 413 637 4507
Email: info@wheatleigh.com
Website: www.wheatleigh.com
www.great-escapes-hotels.com

DIRECTIONS	130 miles (210 km) west of Boston Logan International Airport.
RATES	$$$$
ROOMS	19 suites and guestrooms.
FOOD	Contemporary interpretations of classic French cuisine, served in the elegant main dining room.
HISTORY	Replica 16th century Florentine palazzo built in 1893.
X-FACTOR	Tastefully updated Gilded Age grandeur.

Zeit der Unschuld

Die ersten Superreichen tauchten in Amerika gegen Ende
des 19. Jahrhunderts auf. Sie kontrollierten riesige Summen
und warfen das Geld mit großen Gesten zum Fenster hinaus – so wie es eben Neureiche tun. In den Geschichts-
büchern wird diese Zeit als das Goldene Zeitalter be-
zeichnet. Eine scharfe Beobachterin ihrer Zeit war die
Romanautorin Edith Wharton aus Lenox, Massachusetts.
Nicht weit entfernt von Whartons ehemaligem Zuhause in
Lenox liegt »Wheatleigh«, ein großartiger Landsitz. Es
wurde vom Erben eines Eisenbahn-Tycoons als Kopie eines
florentinischen Palazzos aus dem 16. Jahrhundert als
Hochzeitsgeschenk für seine Tochter erbaut. Die junge
Dame hatte das Geschick, einen echten Grafen aus Spa-
nien zu ehelichen. Für die Holzschnitzereien und Gipser-
arbeiten wurden hundertundfünfzig Handwerker aus
Italien geholt, und der renommierte Landschaftsarchitekt
Frederick Law Olmstead erhielt den Auftrag für das Design
der Gartenanlagen. Heute ist »Wheatleigh« ein Privat-
Resort, das 2000 aufwändig für mehrere Millionen restauriert und dem heutigen Geschmack angepasst wurde. Die
allzu kitschigen Imitationen italienischer Dekors wurden
entfernt und durch zurückhaltende Eleganz in sanften
Tönen ersetzt. Das Hotel-Restaurant mit ausgezeichneter
Weinliste gehört zu den besten der Region und hat sich landesweit einen Namen gemacht. Verliebte Paare und Frisch-
verheiratete finden in »Wheatleigh« ein perfektes Liebes-
nest – kein Wunder: Hier finden immer wieder Hochzeits-
feiern statt.

Buchtipp: »Zeit der Unschuld« von Edith Wharton.
Die Chronik über das Leben der Wohlhabenden in Amerika
im Goldenen Zeitalter.

L'âge de l'innocence

À la fin du 19e siècle, un petit groupe de grands capitalistes
dépensaient sans compter et avec ostentation, à l'instar de
tous les nouveaux riches. Les historiens parlent « d'âge d'or »
de l'Amérique, dont la grande chroniqueuse mondaine fut la
célèbre romancière Edith Wharton, qui partageait son temps
entre New York et Lennox, dans le Massachusetts.
« Weatleigh » se trouve non loin de son ancienne demeure.
Cette gigantesque copie d'un palais florentin du 16e siècle,
une de ces grandioses résidences d'été délirantes emblémati-
ques de l'époque, fut offerte en cadeau de noces par un magnat du chemin de fer à sa fille, bien mariée à un comte
espagnol. Cent cinquante artisans arrivèrent d'Italie pour
réaliser les stucs et les sculptures ; le célèbre paysagiste
américain Frederick Law Olmstead dessina le parc. En 2000,
une coûteuse rénovation la transforma en hôtel de luxe,
dans un style et une atmosphère plus proches de notre propre conception de l'âge d'or. Les touches italianisantes ont
disparu, remplacées par des tons plus doux et des étoffes
d'Orient. Son restaurant et sa cave primée sont connus dans
la région. L'endroit semble avoir été conçu sur-mesure pour
les amoureux et les lunes de miel. De fait, il accueille de
nombreux banquets de mariage. On ne vit peut-être plus à
l'âge de l'innocence, mais on peut la retrouver le temps d'un
week-end à « Weatleigh».

Livre à emporter : « L'Âge de l'innocence » d'Edith Wharton.
La chronique de la vie parmi les riches pendant l'âge d'or de
l'Amérique.

ANREISE	210 km westlich vom internationalen Flughafen Boston Logan.
PREISE	$$$$
ZIMMER	19 Suiten und Gästezimmer.
KÜCHE	Klassisch französische Küche, neu interpretiert, im eleganten Speisesaal serviert.
GESCHICHTE	Replika eines florentinischen Palazzos von 1893 aus dem 16. Jahrhundert.
X-FAKTOR	Geschmackvolle Grandezza auf die heutige Zeit getrimmt.

ACCÈS	À 210 km à l'ouest de l'aéroport international Boston Logan.
PRIX	$$$$
CHAMBRES	19 suites et chambres.
RESTAURATION	Interprétation contemporaine de classiques de la gastronomie française, servie dans l'élégante salle à manger principale.
HISTOIRE	Réplique d'un palais florentin du 16e siècle construit en 1893.
LE « PETIT PLUS »	La grandeur de l'âge d'or élégamment remise au goût du jour.

Sand's End...
Land's End Inn, Provincetown

Sand's End

Provincetown, Massachusetts, is a small town built on a skinny finger of sand that sticks out like a hook in the Atlantic Ocean. It is one of the places in America – Key West in Florida is the other – where the road comes to an end at the sea, where the only way to leave (besides sailing away) is to turn around and go back. "A man may stand there and put all America behind him," Henry David Thoreau wrote about Provincetown in 1865. End-of-the-road towns are magnets for free spirits. Thoreau was just one of a legion of writers, artists, intellectuals and thinkers who have made Provincetown their home. The town, indeed, is a genuine bohemian colony, with a well-regarded local theater, art galleries, writer's workshops, and a big and lively gay community. Eugene O'Neill produced plays here; Norman Mailer retired here. The Land's End Inn, which sits atop a hill overlooking the Atlantic at the far end of town, is the embodiment of Provincetown's free spirit. It is a strange folly of a building, with a rounded main section that looks like the prow of a ship heading out to sea. Inside are quirky rooms – a few, like the domed "Tower Room" are circular, with sweeping views of shoreline. All are decorated with an explosion of Victoriana and fine European linens and fabrics. There are decks and porches where you balance a cocktail on the flat arm of an Adirondack chair and admire the sunset; or scramble down the stairway that leads to the beach. The shops and galleries, and the free spirits who make Provincetown such a unique place, are just a short stroll away from the Land's End Inn. And America? When you're ready you can turn around and go back there.

Book to Pack: "Land's End: A Walk in Provincetown" by Michael Cunningham.
Travel essays on Provincetown by the Pulitzer Prize winning author of "The Hours".

Land's End Inn	**DIRECTIONS** 120 miles drive (195 km) from Boston Logan International Airport.
22 Commercial Street	**RATES** $$
Provincetown, MA 02657	**ROOMS** 16 rooms and suites.
USA	**FOOD** Continental breakfast only; no restaurant (but lots of choices in Provincetown).
Tel. +1 508 487 0706	
Fax +1 508 487 0755	**HISTORY** House was built as a summer cottage by a Boston hatmaker in 1904; later it was converted to an inn which opened in 1926.
Email: info@landsendinn.com	
Website: www.landsendinn.com	**X-FACTOR** Windswept folly of a house, the perfect place to soak up Provincetown's artsy, bohemian mood.
www.great-escapes-hotels.com	

Am Ende der Welt

Die schmale Sandbank ragt wie ein Haken hinaus in den Atlantik. Zuvorderst an der Spitze liegt das Städtchen Provincetown, Massachusetts, dessen Hauptstraße direkt ins Meer mündet. Ausufernde Straßen gibt es sonst nur noch in Key West, Florida. Will man von da weg, hat man nicht gerade viel Möglichkeiten. Entweder man kehrt um – oder man segelt auf dem Meer davon. »An diesem Ort lässt man Amerika ganz hinter sich«, schrieb der Dichter Henry David Thoreau 1865 über Provincetown. Thoreau war nur einer von vielen Schriftstellern, Künstlern, Intellektuellen und Denkern, die von Provincetown magisch angezogen wurden und daraus eine Künstlerkolonie gemacht haben. Es gibt ein angesehenes Theater, Kunstgalerien, Schriftsteller-Workshops und eine lebendige Schwulenszene. Der Bühnendichter und Nobelpreisträger Eugene O'Neill ließ hier seine Stücke aufführen, und Schriftsteller Norman Mailer setzte sich in Provincetown zur Ruhe. Das »Land's End Inn«, eine skurrile Anhäufung verschiedener Häuser, liegt auf einem Hügel hoch über dem Altlantik, am Ende der Stadt. Und wie ein Schiffsbug ragt das Hauptgebäude zum Ozean hinaus. Die Zimmer sind eigenwillig und mit viktorianischer Opulenz eingerichtet, zum Teil haben sie wie im »Tower Room« abgerundete Decken, und die Wäsche ist aus feinstem europäischen Leinen. Abends kann man auf den Terrassen und Veranden des Hotels bei einem Cocktail den Sonnenuntergang genießen. Und wer ein Stück echtes Provincetown erleben möchte, klettert die Treppe hinunter zum Strand oder stöbert durch die typischen Läden und Galerien.

Buchtipp: »Land's End« von Michael Cunningham.
Reise-Essays über Provincetown des Pulitzer-Preisträgers und Autoren von »Die Stunden« (»The Hours«).

Au bout du monde

Provincetown, dans le Massachusetts, est bâtie sur une fine langue de sable qui pointe dans l'Atlantique. C'est l'un de ces endroits des États-unis (comme Key West, en Floride) où la route s'arrête sur l'océan. Le seul moyen d'en repartir est de faire demi-tour (ou de mettre les voiles). « L'homme qui se tient là a toute l'Amérique derrière lui », a écrit Henry D. Thoreau en 1865. Ces villes du bout du monde attirent les libres penseurs. Outre Thoreau, des légions d'artistes, d'écrivains et d'intellectuels se sont établies ici. Une vraie colonie bohème s'y épanouit, avec un théâtre renommé, des galeries d'art, des ateliers d'écriture et une communauté gay très active. Eugène O'Neill y a écrit des pièces, Norman Mailer s'y est retiré. Le « Land's End Inn », perché sur une colline qui domine l'océan, est l'incarnation de l'esprit libre de « Provincetown ». Cette étrange folie au corps arrondi évoque la proue d'un navire mettant le cap vers le large. Certaines chambres, telle que la « Tower Room », circulaire et surmontée d'un dôme, jouissent d'une vue panoramique sur le rivage. Toutes sont décorées à la victorienne avec du beau linge et des étoffes d'Europe. Depuis les terrasses et les porches, on peut poser son cocktail sur l'accoudoir plat d'un fauteuil de l'Adirondack pour admirer le coucher de soleil, à moins qu'on préfère descendre les quelques marches qui mènent à la plage. Les boutiques, les galeries et l'ambiance qui font de « Provincetown » un lieu unique ne sont qu'à un jet de pierre. Et l'Amérique ? Quand vous sentirez prêt, vous n'aurez qu'à pivoter sur vos talons et y retourner.

Livre à emporter : « La Maison du bout du monde » de Michael Cunningham.
Chronique de la vie de deux marginaux dans les années 1980 à la recherche d'un refuge, par l'auteur de « Les Heures », lauréat du prix Pulitzer.

ANREISE	195 km vom internationalen Flughafen Boston Logan.
PREISE	$$
ZIMMER	16 Zimmer und Suiten.
KÜCHE	Kontinentales Frühstück; kein Restaurant (aber eine große Auswahl an Restaurants in Provincetown).
GESCHICHTE	1904 als Sommer-Cottage von einem Hutmacher aus Boston erbaut, ab 1926 ein Gasthaus.
X-FAKTOR	Das etwas skurrile Hotel ist der perfekte Ort, um die Künstlerseele von Provincetown zu entdecken.

ACCÈS	À 195 Km de l'aéroport international Boston Logan.
PRIX	$$
CHAMBRES	16 chambres et suites.
RESTAURATION	Petit-déjeuner continental uniquement ; pas de restaurant (mais il n'en manque pas à Provincetown).
HISTOIRE	Ancienne résidence d'été construite par un chapelier de Boston en 1904 ; convertie en auberge en 1926.
LE « PETIT PLUS »	Folie battue par les vents ; l'endroit idéal pour tremper dans l'ambiance bohème et artistique de Provincetown.

A Rose is a Rose...
The Wauwinet, Nantucket

A Rose is a Rose

Siasconset – pronounced "Skon-set" by the locals – is at the far end of Nantucket Island from the town, and from the ferry pier. Quiet and low, the fishing village faces eastwards, towards the endless sea and Europe beyond. Nantucket is known for its grey-shingled cottages, covered with vines of pink roses, which were originally built by the sea captains and sailors who moved here during the 1800s, when whale oil was a prized commodity. Whaling ships sailed out into the cold Atlantic Ocean, sometimes for months. Back then, Nantucket was a wealthy place, but life was not always rose-covered: many of the cottages had a tiny cupola on the roof, ringed by a railing, so that nervous sea captain's wives could look out to sea and try to spot approaching ships – and ship-wrecks (the cupolas were called "widow's walks"). After the invention of electric lighting, Nantucket's commercial life faded and was replaced by tourism; it was, famously, a summer retreat for America's "old money" families. There were few hotels or inns in the main village, and in Siasconset only one, the Wauwinet. Remodelled and reopened as an exclusive inn in 1988, the Wauwinet has preserved the charm of a way of life that is disappearing, as Nantucket's real estate development runs rampant. Peaceful, its garden bursting with flowers, it commands amazing views from its location between two private beaches, one on the Atlantic and one on Nantucket Bay. A wildlife preserve is right next door, so the birdwatching from the white wicker chairs on the front lawn is excellent. Inside the rooms are pretty and filled with sunlight and good books; the restaurant downstairs, Topper's, is among the best on the island. Whether you arrange a sail, a picnic, or a boat trip into town, worldly cares will fade into the distance. From the Wauwinet, life seems covered in roses.

Book to Pack: "Moby Dick" by Herman Melville.
The fabled quest for the great white whale captures the atmosphere of Nantucket in its heyday.

The Wauwinet
120 Wauwinet Road
Nantucket, MA 02584
USA
Tel. +1 508 228 0145
Fax +1 508 325 0657
Email: email@wauwinet.com
Website: www.wauwinet.com
www.great-escapes-hotels.com

DIRECTIONS	On Nantucket Island, 9 miles (15 km) from Nantucket Town.
RATES	$$$
ROOMS	35 rooms and cottages.
FOOD	Fine dining, emphasis on local seafood at Topper's restaurant, open for breakfast, lunch and dinner.
HISTORY	Originally the Wauwinet House, an inn opened in the mid-1900s. Property remodelled in 1988.
X-FACTOR	Charm, squared: the quintessential rose-covered Nantucket cottage.

Eine Rose ist eine Rose

Siasconset (»Skon-set« ausgesprochen) am östlichen Ende von Nantucket Island, Massachusetts, liegt abgelegen. Vom stillen Fischerdorf mit den typischen rosenüberwachsenen, grauen Schindel-Cottages kann man den Blick übers weite Meer schweifen lassen. Die Cottages wurden im 19. Jahrhundert von Seeleuten gebaut, die nach Nantucket zogen, um ihr Glück zu suchen. Damals blühte der Handel mit Walfischöl, und mit ihren Schiffen segelten sie zum Walfang hinaus in den kalten Atlantik. Manchmal blieben sie monatelang auf hoher See. Die Ehefrauen der Seeleute bangten um das Leben ihrer Männer und guckten bange durch die kleinen Kuppeln auf den Dächern der Cottages, um die ankommenden Schiffe zu erspähen. Statt stolzer Schiffe sahen sie manchmal auch Wracks ankommen. Deshalb werden die Kuppeln auch »Witwengänge« genannt. Mit dem Aufkommen der Elektrizität veränderte sich Nantucket. Aus der Fischerinsel wurde ein Touristenort. Vor allem wohlhabende Familien reisten zur Sommerfrische nach Nantucket. Erste Hotels wurden gebaut wie das »Wauwinet« in Siasconset. 1988 wurde es umgebaut und als exklusives Gasthaus wiedereröffnet. Der Immobilienboom der letzten Jahrzehnte hat das Gesicht der Insel verändert, doch das »Wauwinet« hat noch immer den Charme von früher. Es liegt zwischen zwei Privatstränden, neben einem Naturschutzgebiet inmitten eines blühenden Garten, und der Blick auf die Nantucket Bay ist so zauberhaft wie die lichtdurchfluteten Zimmer. Der schönste Zeitvertrieb in Nantucket: Segeln oder Picknicks. Was man auch unternimmt, der Alltag erscheint wunderbar weit weg.

Buchtipp: »Moby Dick« von Herman Melville.
Die Fabel über die Suche nach dem großen weißen Walfisch beschreibt die Atmosphäre des alten Nantucket.

Une rose est une rose

Siasconet (prononcez « Skon-set ») se trouve à l'autre bout de la ville et du débarcadère de Nantucket. Ce paisible village de pêcheurs fait face à l'océan et à l'Europe. L'île est connue pour ses cottages aux bardeaux gris couverts de rosiers grimpants construits par des marins au début du 19e siècle quand l'huile de baleine était une denrée précieuse. Les baleiniers s'aventuraient dans l'Atlantique glacé pendant des mois. Nantucket était alors prospère mais la vie n'y était pas toujours rose. Bon nombre de cottages sont surmontés d'une coupole ceinte d'une rambarde (une « promenade de veuve ») d'où les femmes de capitaines scrutaient l'horizon pour repérer les navires rentrant... ou les naufrages. Avec l'avènement de l'électricité, le commerce a cédé le pas au tourisme. Les vieilles fortunes d'Amérique établirent ici leurs résidences d'été. L'île ne compte qu'une poignée d'hôtels et Siasconet un seul, le « Wauwinet ». Rénové en 1988, tranquille et entouré d'un jardin fleuri, il conserve le charme d'un mode de vie en voie d'extinction tandis que sévit le développement immobilier. Situé entre deux plages, l'une sur l'Atlantique, l'autre sur la baie de Nantucket, il jouit de vues spectaculaires. Depuis les fauteuils en osier blanc sur la pelouse, on peut observer les oiseaux de la réserve naturelle tout à côté. Ses jolies chambres claires sont remplies de bons livres. Son restaurant, « Topper's », est un des meilleurs de l'île. Que vous envisagiez une promenade en mer, un pique-nique ou une virée en ville, vos soucis s'envoleront car, au « Wauwinet ». la vie semble un tapis de roses.

Livre à emporter : « Moby Dick » d'Herman Melville.
La quête fabuleuse de la grande baleine blanche restitue fort bien l'atmosphère de la grande époque de Nantucket.

ANREISE	15 km vom Hauptort Nantucket.
PREISE	$$$
ZIMMER	35 Zimmer und Cottages.
KÜCHE	Das Gourmetrestaurant »Topper's« mit lokalen Fischspezialitäten gehört zu den besten der Insel. Morgens, mittags und abends geöffnet.
GESCHICHTE	Mitte des 20. Jahrhunderts als Gasthaus »Wauwinet House« gebaut. 1988 renoviert.
X-FAKTOR	Nantucket-Charme mit typischen rosenbedeckten Schindel-Cottages.

ACCÈS	Sur l'île de Nantucket, à 15 km de la ville de Nantucket.
PRIX	$$$
CHAMBRES	35 chambres et cottages.
RESTAURATION	Le restaurant « Topper's », ouvert pour le déjeuner et le dîner, propose une bonne cuisine avec des spécialités à base des produits de la mer locaux.
HISTOIRE	Initialement connue comme la « Wauwinet House », une auberge ouverte vers le milieu du 20e siècle, rénovée en 1988.
LE « PETIT PLUS »	Le charme bien ordonné, la quintessence du cottage fleuri de Nantucket.

Long, Lazy Days...
The Moorings Village, Islamorada

Long, Lazy Days

This is what Florida used to be like, before the tourists arrived in force, before real estate speculators turned vast stretches of beach into concrete walls of condominums. At Moorings Village, an 18 acre compound of little cottages and houses small and grand in Islamorada, Florida, things are kept deliberately simple. There is no fancy restaurant – each of the homes is self-contained, with a kitchen and in many cases a washer and dryer. There are no "activities" scheduled, but a 1,100 foot (333 metre) long private white sand beach is at the guest's disposal for kayaking, windsurfing, swimming, or just lazing around. Moorings Village has a variety of lodgings; some are modest bungalows with screened porches that look like the setting for a scene in a crime thriller by famous Florida authors Carl Hiassen or Elmore Leonard; others are neat two-story colonial houses with pillars and gingerbread and wraparound porches. All are placed well away from the beach, ensuring its quiet and beauty. Islamorada is the US capital of the sport of bonefishing, which has nothing to do with bones, but rather involves chasing one of the most difficult to catch and vigorously aggressive deep sea fish in North America. Here in the peaceful, sleepy Moorings Village, the bonefish are probably the most rambunctious creatures you'll encounter.

Book to pack: "Tourist Season" by Carl Hiaasen.
Biting satire about Florida life, full of local color and characters.

The Moorings Village
123 Beach Road
Islamorada, FL 33036
USA
Tel. +1 305 664 4708
Fax +1 305 664 4242
Website: www.themooringsvillage.com
www.great-escapes-hotels.com

DIRECTIONS	80 miles (130 km) south of Miami International Airport.
RATES	$$$
ROOMS	18 cottages and houses, ranging from one to three bedrooms.
FOOD	Self-catering: the houses and cottages have fully-equipped kitchens.
HISTORY	Originally built in 1936 as a private estate. Opened as a resort in 1989.
X-FACTOR	Discover a rare bit of old Florida, before the real estate and tourism boom.

Nichts als Faulenzen

»Moorings Village« ist ein Stück Florida, wie es früher einmal war. Bevor Touristenströme einfielen, Immobilienspekulanten Wohnsiedlungen hinklotzten und Betonwüsten aus Stränden machten. Die 7,2 Hektar große Siedlung auf Islamorada besteht aus kleinen Cottages und verschiedenen größeren und kleineren Häusern. Der Lifestyle ist bewusst einfach, ein schickes Restaurant sucht man hier vergebens. Jedes der Häuser ist aber mit einer Küche ausgestattet, und die meisten verfügen auch über eine Waschmaschine und einen Wäschetrockner. »Moorings Village« bietet den Gästen auch kein ausgeklügeltes Programm mit Aktivitäten an, doch langweilig wird hier niemandem. Am über 300 Meter langen, weißen Privatstrand kann man kajakfahren, surfen, schwimmen oder ganz einfach faulenzen. Die Unterkünfte sind sehr unterschiedlich: hier die bescheidenen Bungalows mit Veranden und Storen, die an Szenerien erinnern, wie sie Floridas bekannteste Krimiautoren, Carl Hiaasen und Elmore Leonard, beschreiben. Dort die schmucken zweistöckigen Kolonialhäuser mit säulenverzierten Veranden. Alle liegen, lauschig und ruhig, etwas weiter weg vom Strand. Islamorada ist übrigens das Mekka einer sehr exklusiven Sportart: dem »Bonefishing«. Hier wird Jagd nach aggressiven Riesenbarschen gemacht. Ein bisschen Aufregung kann auch im sonst friedlichen und verschlafenen »Moorings Village« nicht schaden.

Buchtipp: »Miami-Terror« von Carl Hiaasen.
Bissige Satire über das Leben in Florida mit viel Lokalkolorit.

De longues journées de paresse

C'est à cela que ressemblait la Floride avant l'arrivée en masse des touristes, quand les spéculateurs immobiliers n'avaient pas encore bétonné de vastes étendues de plages pour y construire des immeubles d'appartements. À Islamorada, « Moorings Village » est un domaine de plus de sept hectares où la vie est maintenue délibérément simple. Ici, pas de restaurant branché. Chacune des maisons est autosuffisante, avec sa cuisine et, dans la plupart des cas, tout l'équipement ménager nécessaire. Il n'y pas d'activités prévues, rien qu'une plage privée de sable blanc de plus de 300 mètres de long, où l'on peut faire du kayac, de la planche à voile, nager ou rien du tout. « Moorings Village » possède tout un éventail de logements : du modeste bungalow avec son porche et sa moustiquaire, semblant tout droit sorti d'un polar des célèbres auteurs Carl Hiassen ou Elmore Leonard (tous deux de Floride), à la demeure coloniale avec ses balcons ouvragés, ses colonnes et sa galerie ouverte qui court tout autour de la maison. Tous les bâtiments sont construits en retrait de la plage pour préserver son calme et sa beauté.
Islamorada est la capitale américaine de la pêche à la banane de mer, ou « bonefishing », qui n'a rien à voir avec le fruit du bananier mais avec la chasse de l'un des poissons de haute mer les plus vigoureux et agressifs d'Amérique du Nord. À « Moorings Village », la banane de mer est sans doute la créature la plus énervée que vous croiserez.

Livre à emporter : « Miami Park » de Carl Hiaasen.
Satire acerbe de la vie en Floride, remplie de personnages hauts en couleurs.

ANREISE	130 km südlich vom internationalen Flughafen in Miami.	
PREISE	$$$	
ZIMMER	Insgesamt 18 Cottages und Häuser mit ein bis drei Schlafzimmern.	
KÜCHE	Selbstversorgung; die Häuser und Cottages verfügen über eine Küche.	
GESCHICHTE	1936 als Privatanlage gebaut. Seit 1989 ein Resort.	
X-FAKTOR	Florida wie es früher war.	

ACCÈS	À 130 km au sud de l'aéroport international de Miami.
PRIX	$$$
CHAMBRES	18 bungalows et maisons, comptant de une à trois chambres à coucher.
RESTAURATION	Les maisons et les bungalows ont des cuisines entièrement équipées.
HISTOIRE	Construit en 1936 comme un domaine privé. Converti en complexe hôtelier en 1989.
LE « PETIT PLUS »	Découvrez un des rares vestiges de la Floride d'autrefois, avant le boom du tourisme et de l'immobilier.

Your Own Key...
Little Palm Island, Little Torch Key

Little Palm Island,
Little Torch Key

Your Own Key

As you drive south from Miami on US 1, the road narrows to
a two lane highway, one of the most dramatic stretches of
road in the country. The highway is actually a long causeway
that seems to leapfrog over open ocean, as it passes through
one small sandy island after another. This chain of little
islands, the Florida Keys, is the southernmost point in the
United States, and as you continue southward, it often feels
as if you are going to drive right off the edge of the continent. The air is thick and humid, the landscape wild. Birds
and waterfowl swoop overhead – the Everglades National
Park is close by – and, occasionally in the early mornings,
shy little deer the size of dogs (Key Deer, an endangered spe-
cies) feed by the roadside.
Little Palm Island resort is located on Little Torch Key a private island accessible only by the launch that carries guests
over to the resort from the mainland. It is just three miles
offshore, but it feels a million miles away. The resort boasts
twenty eight varieties of lush palm trees, white sand beaches, aquamarine ocean – and no cellphones, televisions or
clocks to spoil the illusion that you have washed up in
Tonga, or Fiji. There are twenty eight large seaside cottages,
decorated in one of three tropical themes: Indonesian, Poly-
nesian, British Colonial. Whichever you choose, you can be
sure it will have a king bed draped in billowy mosquito net-
ting, the fragrance of jasmine, the sound of birds, and solitude.

Book to pack: "The Empty Copper Sea" by John D. MacDonald.
A murder potboiler set in the Keys by Florida's most renowned noir thriller writer.

Little Palm Island Resort & Spa
28500 Overseas Highway
Little Torch Key, FL 33042
USA
Tel. +1 305 515 4004
Fax +1 305 515 4843
Email: getlost@littlepalmisland.com
Website: www.littlepalmisland.com
www.great-escapes-hotels.com

DIRECTIONS	Located on Little Torch Key, an island about 125 miles (200 km) south of Miami International Airport. Access to the island is by private plane or boat only.
RATES	$$$$
ROOMS	28 thatched-roof oceanfront bungalows and two grand suites.
FOOD	The Dining Room restaurant serves "Floribbean" cuisine – elegantly presented local seafood specialties.
HISTORY	A private island that used to belong to a Florida politician. Converted in 1988 to a private resort.
X-FACTOR	Lush Caribbean-like tropical solitude, without leaving the continental USA.

Reif für die Insel

Die US 1 mündet südlich von Miami in eine schmale, zwei-
spurige Überlandstraße und gehört zu den zauberhaftesten
Straßenstrecken des Landes. Eigentlich ein langer Damm,
reiht sie über den offenen Ozean hinweg kleine, sandige
Inseln zu einer Kette auf. Die Florida Keys bilden den süd-
lichsten Punkt der Vereinigten Staaten, und wer auf dem
Damm weiter in diese Richtung fährt, glaubt gleich über
den Horizont zu kippen. Die Luft ist schwer und feucht, die
Landschaft wild. Im Sturzflug rasen einem Vögel über den
Kopf – der »Everglades National Park« ist in der Nähe –, und
manchmal kann man am frühen Morgen fressendes »Key
Deer« am Straßenrand beobachten, ein vor dem Aussterben
bedrohtes Kleinwild, das nicht größer ist als ein Hund.
Das Resort »Little Palm Island« auf der Privatinsel »Little
Torch Key« ist nur per Schiff zu erreichen. Die Strecke ist
zwar nur knapp fünf Kilometer lang, doch man hat das
Gefühl, tausende von Kilometern weit weg zu sein. Im
Resort zeigen dann 28 verschiedene üppige Palmenarten,
weiße Sandstrände und der aquamarine Ozean ihre ganze
Pracht, sodass man sich auf Tonga oder Fidschi glaubt.
Weder Handys, Fernseher noch Uhren stören diese Illusion.
Entsprechend sind auch die 28 großzügigen Strand-Cottages
eingerichtet: im indonesischen, polynesischen oder britischen Kolonialstil. In den Cottages stehen große Kingsize-
Doppelbetten, die in Moskitonetze eingehüllt sind. Überall
schwebt der Duft von Jasminblüten, und einzig der Gesang
der Vögel durchbricht die Ruhe.

Buchtipp: »Der dunkelschwarze Betrug« von John D. MacDonald.
Kriminalroman aus der Feder des bekanntesten Thriller-
Autors Floridas.

Une île rien que pour vous

Quand vous descendez l'US1 vers le sud à partir de Miami,
la chaussée rétrécit pour former la route à deux voies la plus
spectaculaire du pays. Elle devient en fait une longue passe-
relle qui semble jouer à saute-mouton sur l'océan ouvert,
rebondissant d'une île sablonneuse à l'autre. Cette chaîne
d'îlots, les « Keys » de Floride, constitue le point le plus
méridional des États-Unis. À mesure que l'on avance, on a
l'impression qu'on va tomber du bout du continent. L'air est
lourd et humide, les paysages sont luxuriants. Le « parc
national des Everglades » est tout près : les oiseaux abondent
et parfois, le matin, on voit de petits cervidés de la taille d'un
chien (les cerfs des Keys, une espèce en voie de disparition)
brouter sur le bord de la route.
« Little Palm Island » est située sur « Little Torch Key », une
île privée accessible uniquement par la vedette de l'hôtel qui
fait la navette avec la terre ferme. Elle ne se trouve qu'à cinq
kilomètres environ de la côte mais semble perdue au milieu
de nulle part. L'établissement est fier de ses vingt-huit espè-
ces de palmiers, de ses plages de sable blanc, de son eau tur-
quoise et aucun téléphone portable, poste de télévision ni
pendule ne viennent gâcher l'illusion d'avoir échoué sur les
rivages de Tonga ou de Fiji. Les vingt-huit grands bungalows
qui donnent sur la mer sont décorés dans un thème tropical :
indonésien, polynésien ou colonial britannique. Quel que
soit votre choix, vous pouvez compter sur un grand lit drapé
d'une ample moustiquaire, le parfum du jasmin, le chant
des oiseaux et la solitude.

Livre à emporter : « Le combat pour l'île » de John D. MacDonald.
Une histoire de meurtre située dans les Keys, par le plus
célèbre des auteurs de polars de Floride.

ANREISE	Etwa 200 km südlich vom internationalen Flughafen Miami. Nur mit einem Privatflugzeug oder per Schiff zu erreichen.
PREISE	$$$$
ZIMMER	28 Strand-Bungalows mit Strohdächern, zwei große Suiten.
KÜCHE	Restaurant mit »Floribbean« Küche – elegant präsentier- te Seafood-Spezialitäten.
GESCHICHTE	Die Privatinsel gehörte einem lokalen Politiker. 1988 wurde daraus ein Resort.
X-FAKTOR	Abgeschiedenheit in üppiger, tropischer Karibik- Landschaft.

ACCÈS	L'île de « Little Torch Key », se trouve à environ 200 km au sud de l'aéroport international de Miami. On accè- de uniquement par avion ou bateau privé.
PRIX	$$$$
CHAMBRES	28 bungalows avec un toit en chaume donnant sur l'o- céan et deux grandes suites.
RESTAURATION	Le restaurant propose une cuisine « floribéenne »: des spécialités de poissons et fruits de mer élégamment présentées.
HISTOIRE	Une île privée qui appartenait autrefois à un politicien de Floride. Convertie en hôtel en 1988.
LE « PETIT PLUS »	Une tranquillité tropicale absolue.

Texas Modern...
Hotel San José, Austin

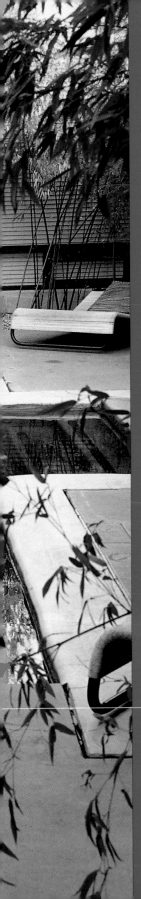

Texas Modern

For Americans, Austin has a reputation as the best place in Texas to have fun – the state capital is home to a big university, lots of intellectuals and artists, quirky bohemians and hipsters young and old. Every year the city hosts a major film festival, and an international music-business convention, South by Southwest. Speaking of music, Austin probably has more live musicians per capita than any other city in America, from country to rock to classical, and you can happily spend an entire week cruising nightclubs and concert halls. But if you stay in the Hotel San José, Austin's coolest hotel, you may not make it out of the parking lot. The San José Hotel is one of those happy little accidents of a hotel where a structure with bones and history fell into the hands of an owner with taste and style. Built in the 1930s as a classic American motor hotel, it fell into disrepair over the years. It was a flophouse, then a Bible school. Then native Texan Liz Lambert bought it in the 1990s, and saved up until she could afford to renovate it exactly as she wanted: as a mimimalist-inspired funky retreat. Rooms are simply furnished with red Eames chairs and platform beds; the floors are cool, polished concrete. By contrast, the grounds and common areas are lush with bamboo, cactus and vine covered arbors; you gravitate, automatically, to the main courtyard, where metal lawn chairs and a little swimming pool tempt you to linger over coffee or wine. But what will make you most happy about staying at the Hotel San José are the details. For instance, the breakfast that comes in a handmade Japanese bento box, and the vintage Remington typewriter and Polaroid camera available from the front desk. Borrow it now, and take a picture of your room in the Hotel San José, to remember the best fun you had in Austin.

Book to Pack: "The Last Picture Show" by Larry McMurtry. Novel about life in a small Texas town by the Pulitzer Prize winning Texas novelist.

Hotel San José	
1316 South Congress Street	
Austin, TX 78704	
USA	
Tel. +1 512 444 7322	
Fax +1 512 444 7362	
Website: www.sanjosehotel.com	
www.great-escapes-hotels.com	

DIRECTIONS	In downtown Austin, 9 miles (15 km) northwest of Austin-Bergstrom International Airport.
RATES	$
ROOMS	40 guest rooms.
FOOD	Free continental breakfast served in room; Jo's, a coffeeshop across the parking lot, serves BBQ sandwiches and salads.
HISTORY	1930's era motor court motel, renovated in 1998.
X-FACTOR	The hippest place to stay in Austin, Texas.

»Texas modern«

Austin, die Hauptstadt von Texas, ist eine äußerst lebendige Stadt. Wie in jeder Universitätsstadt tummeln sich hier Intellektuelle, Künstler und Hipster. Austin kann sogar mit einem alljährlichen Filmfestival aufwarten. Auch die internationale Musikindustrie pilgert regelmäßig in die Stadt, um sich am Kongress »South by Southwest« auszutauschen. Den Ort hätte man für einen solchen Anlass nicht besser erfinden können: Austin hat mehr Live-Musiker – Country, Rock und Klassisch – pro Einwohner als jede andere Stadt Amerikas. Hier kann man eine ganze Woche lang durch Nachtclubs und Konzerthallen ziehen, ohne sich auch nur eine Sekunde zu langweilen. Doch aufgepasst, wer im coolsten Hotel der Stadt, dem »San José«, absteigt, wird es kaum weiter als bis zum Parkplatz schaffen. Das »San José Hotel« hatte das Glück, an eine Besitzerin zu geraten, die für die Architektur und die Geschichte des ehemaligen Motels aus den Dreißigern das richtige Gespür hatte. Lange eine billige Absteige, dann eine Bibelschule, kaufte es die Texanerin Liz Lambert in den Neunzigern, ohne allerdings das Geld zu haben, das baufällige Motel instand zu setzen. Lambert sparte so lange, bis sie sich die Renovierung leisten konnte, die ihr vorschwebte. Die Zimmer mit polierten Betonböden sind schlicht-minimalistisch mit roten Eames-Stühlen und Plattform-Betten eingerichtet. Der Innenhof mit Swimmingpool setzt mit üppigem Bambus, Kakteen und weinumrankten Lauben einen Kontrapunkt. Lamberts Sinn für Stil zeigt sich auch in den Details: Das Frühstück wird zum Beispiel in einer handgefertigten japanischen Bento-Box gereicht.

Buchtipp: »Die letzte Vorstellung« von Larry McMurtry. Roman über das Leben in einer texanischen Kleinstadt vom Pulitzer-Preisträger.

« Texas modern »

Pour les Américains, Austin est la ville du Texas où l'on s'amuse : elle héberge une grande université, une multitude d'intellectuels, d'artistes, d'excentriques et de branchés de tous âges. Chaque année s'y tiennent un grand festival du cinéma et un salon international du disque. De fait, elle compte un nombre impressionnant de musiciens. Country, rock ou classique, on peut passer une semaine à écumer night-clubs et salles de concert. Mais si vous logez à l'« Hotel San José », le plus cool d'Austin, vous n'aurez pas envie de sortir. C'est l'un de ces petits accidents heureux où une structure avec une histoire tombe entre les mains d'une femme de goût. Construit dans les années 30 comme un motel classique, il devint asile de nuit puis école de catéchisme avant d'être ramené à la vie dans les années 1990 par la Texane Liz Lambert, qui épargna jusqu'à pouvoir le restaurer exactement tel qu'elle le voulait : minimaliste et moderne. Les chambres sont meublées de chaises rouges de Eames et de lits sur plateformes. Les sols sont en béton poli. En revanche, jardins et parties communes débordent de bambous, de cactus et de tonnelles envahies par la vigne. On gravite autour de la cour principale, où des transats en métal et une petite piscine invitent à s'attarder pour un café ou un verre de vin. Mais ce qui vous ravira le plus, ce sont les détails. Les petits déjeuners sont servis dans des boîtes artisanales en bentonite ; une vieille Remington et un Polaroïd sont disponibles à la réception. Empruntez-le pour photographier votre chambre en souvenir du bon temps passé à Austin.

Livre à emporter : « La dernière séance » de Larry McMurtry. Roman sur la vie dans une petite ville du Texas par un auteur texan lauréat du prix Pulitzer.

ANREISE	Im Stadtzentrum von Austin, rund 15 km nordwestlich vom internationalen Flughafen Austin-Bergstrom.
PREISE	$
ZIMMER	40 Gästezimmer.
KÜCHE	Ein kontinentales Frühstück ist im Preis inbegriffen und wird direkt aufs Zimmer gebracht. Im Coffeeshop »Jo's« gibt es BBQ Sandwiches und Salate.
GESCHICHTE	Motel aus den Dreißigern, 1998 renoviert.
X-FAKTOR	Das angesagteste Hotel in Austin, Texas.

ACCÈS	Au centre d'Austin, à 15 km au nord-ouest de l'aéroport international d'Austin-Bergstrom.
PRIX	$
CHAMBRES	40 chambres.
RESTAURATION	Petit-déjeuner continental gracieusement offert et servi dans les chambres. De l'autre côté du parking, le café «Jo's» sert des sandwichs au barbecue et des salades.
HISTOIRE	Motel des années 1930, rénové en 1998.
LE « PETiT PLUS »	L'hôtel le plus branché d'Austin, au Texas.

Cowtown Cool...
The Hotel Paisano, Marfa

Cowtown Cool

Marfa, population 2,424, sits on the high desert plateau of West Texas, a good three hours drive from anywhere. Marfa got its start as a "cowtown" in 1883; it was a railroad hub for the local ranchers to ship their cattle up north. But even back then, this was a one-horse town with a touch of class – the wife of the railroad boss who founded the town named it "Marfa" after a character in Dostoevsky's "Brothers Kara-mazov". The original builders of the Hotel Paisano also seem to have had a premonition that big things were in store for little Marfa – the announcement for their grand, faux-Spanish style hotel, constructed just before the 1929 stock market crash proclaimed it "the most elegant hotel be-tween El Paso and San Antonio." In the 1950s, the Paisano, which resembles a cross between a wedding cake and The Alamo, served as the headquarters for the actors and crew of "Giant", an epic film about Texas history starring the late cinema icon James Dean. There's a room filled with Dean memorabilia now at the hotel, which was gently renovated in 2001, but still feels like a place where you could make a deal in the lobby for 1,000 head of cattle over whiskey and cigars. But the hip travellers who keep Hotel Paisano's 33 rooms fully-booked year round are not here to pay homage to Dean, Dostoyevsky, nor cows. They are here to visit the Chinati Foundation, artist Donald Judd's museum of site-specific sculpture, and the engine behind the Hotel Paisano's – and Marfa's – unexpected renaissance.

Book to Pack: "Giant" by Edna Ferber.

The book from which the James Dean movie was made; a sweeping tale of Texas history by a famous 1920's American novelist.

The Hotel Paisano
P.O. Box Z
Marfa, TX 79843
USA
Tel. +1 432 729 3669
Fax +1 432 729 3779
Email: frontdesk.hp@sbcglobal.net
Website: www.hotelpaisano.com
www.great-escapes-hotels.com

DIRECTIONS	190 miles (300 km) southeast of El Paso International Airport.
RATES	$
ROOMS	33 rooms.
FOOD	Jett's Grill-named after James Dean's character in "Giant": steaks, ribs, chops, live music on weekends.
HISTORY	Originally built as a grand hotel in 1929; renovated and reopened in 2001.
X-FACTOR	Historic Spanish stucco hotel with a dash of old Hollywood glamour.

Im Schatten der Giganten

Marfa liegt hoch auf einem Wüstenplateau im Westen von Texas – im Niemandsland. Die nächste größere Stadt, El Paso, ist etwa drei Autostunden entfernt. Marfa hat gerade mal 2424 Einwohner. Der Ort wurde 1883 gegründet und war auch damals nicht viel größer als ein »Kuhdorf«. Die Haupttätigkeit der Rancher bestand darin, Vieh in Bahnwaggons zu verfrachten und es Richtung Norden transportieren zu lassen. Ein Hauch von Klasse brachte die Gattin des Eisenbahn-Chefs in den gottverlassenen Ort. Sie nannte ihn »Marfa« nach einer Figur aus Dostojewskis »Die Brüder Karamasow«. Kurz vor dem großen Börsencrash 1929 wurde in Marfa das »Hotel Paisano« im spanischen Kolonialstil eröffnet und stolz als »elegantestes Hotel zwischen El Paso und San Antonio« beworben. Vielleicht eine kleine Vorahnung auf eine größere Zukunft. Das Hotel, das aussieht wie eine Kreuzung aus einer Hochzeitstorte und der Festung »The Alamo«, stand zum ersten Mal in den Fünfzigern im Rampenlicht. Die Crew von »Giant«, einem Film über die Geschichte von Texas, hatte sich hier einquartiert. Darunter Hollywood-Ikone James Dean. Eines der Hotelzimmer dient heute als Dean-Museum. Das »Paisano« wurde 2001 sanft renoviert, aber noch immer kann man sich vorstellen, wie in der Lobby bei Whisky und Zigarren ein Kuhhandel nach dem anderen abgeschlossen wurde. Heute sind die Hotelgäste allerdings weder an Kühen noch an James Dean interessiert. Sie kommen der Chinati Foundation wegen. Das Museum mit Skulpturen und Installationen des Künstlers Donald Judd ist heute der Grund, nach Marfa zu reisen.

Buchtipp: »Giganten« von Edna Ferber.

Eine Erzählung aus dem historischen Texas. Das Buch, in den 1920ern verfasst, diente als Vorlage für den gleichnamigen Film mit James Dean.

Dans l'ombre des géants

Marfa, 2 424 habitants, est perchée sur un haut plateau dans le désert de l'ouest texan, à trois bonnes heures de nulle part. Elle a vu le jour en 1883 comme gare d'où les ranchers venaient envoyer leurs troupeaux vers le nord. Mais, même alors, c'était un bled perdu avec un petit quelque chose en plus : la femme du chef des chemins de fer qui fonda le bourg le baptisa « Marfa » en hommage à un personnage des « Frères Karamazov » de Dostoïevski. Les bâtisseurs du « Paisano » devaient avoir pressenti l'avenir grandiose du petit bourg : la publicité de leur grand hôtel au style hispanisant, construit juste avant le krach de 1929, le proclamait « l'établissement le plus élégant entre El Paso et San Antonio ». Dans les années cinquante, le Paisano, un hybride entre une pièce montée et « l'Alamo », servit de Q. G. aux acteurs et à l'équipe « de Géants », film à grand spectacle qui retrace une partie de l'histoire du Texas avec le légendaire James Dean. Une chambre abrite aujourd'hui tous les souvenirs de la star. L'hôtel a été restauré en 2001 mais, dans le hall, on peut encore s'imaginer troquant 1 000 têtes de bétail contre du whisky et des cigares. Toutefois, les voyageurs éclairés qui remplissent l'hôtel toute l'année ne viennent ni pour Dean, ni pour Dostoïevski ni pour les vaches. Ils sont là pour visiter la fondation « Chinati », le musée de sculptures contextuelles créé par Donald Judd, le moteur derrière la renaissance inattendue de l'« Hotel Paisano » et de Marfa.

Livre à emporter : « Géant » d'Edna Ferber.

Le livre qui a inspiré le film avec James Dean, tout un pan de l'histoire du Texas par la célèbre romancière américaine des années vingt.

ANREISE	300 km südöstlich vom internationalen Flughafen El Paso.
PREISE	$
ZIMMER	33 Zimmer.
KÜCHE	Der »Jett's Grill« ist nach der von James Dean gespielten Figur im Film »Die Giganten« benannt. Hier gibt's Steaks, Ribs, Chops und am Wochenende wird Live-Musik gespielt.
GESCHICHTE	1929 als Grand-Hotel gebaut, 2001 renoviert und wiedereröffnet.
X-FAKTOR	Historisches Hotel im spanischen Kolonialstil mit einem Hauch Hollywood-Glamour.

ACCÈS	À 300 km au sud-est de l'aéroport international d'El Paso.
PRIX	$
CHAMBRES	33 chambres.
RESTAURATION	Le « Jett's Grill », baptisé d'après le personnage de James Dean dans « Géant » : steaks, côtes de bœuf, côtelettes ; musique live les week-ends.
HISTOIRE	Construit comme un « grand hôtel » en 1929, restauré et rouvert en 2001.
LE « PETIT PLUS »	Hôtel historique rococo avec une pointe de vieux glamour hollywoodien.

Cowboy Minimalist...
Thunderbird Motel, Marfa

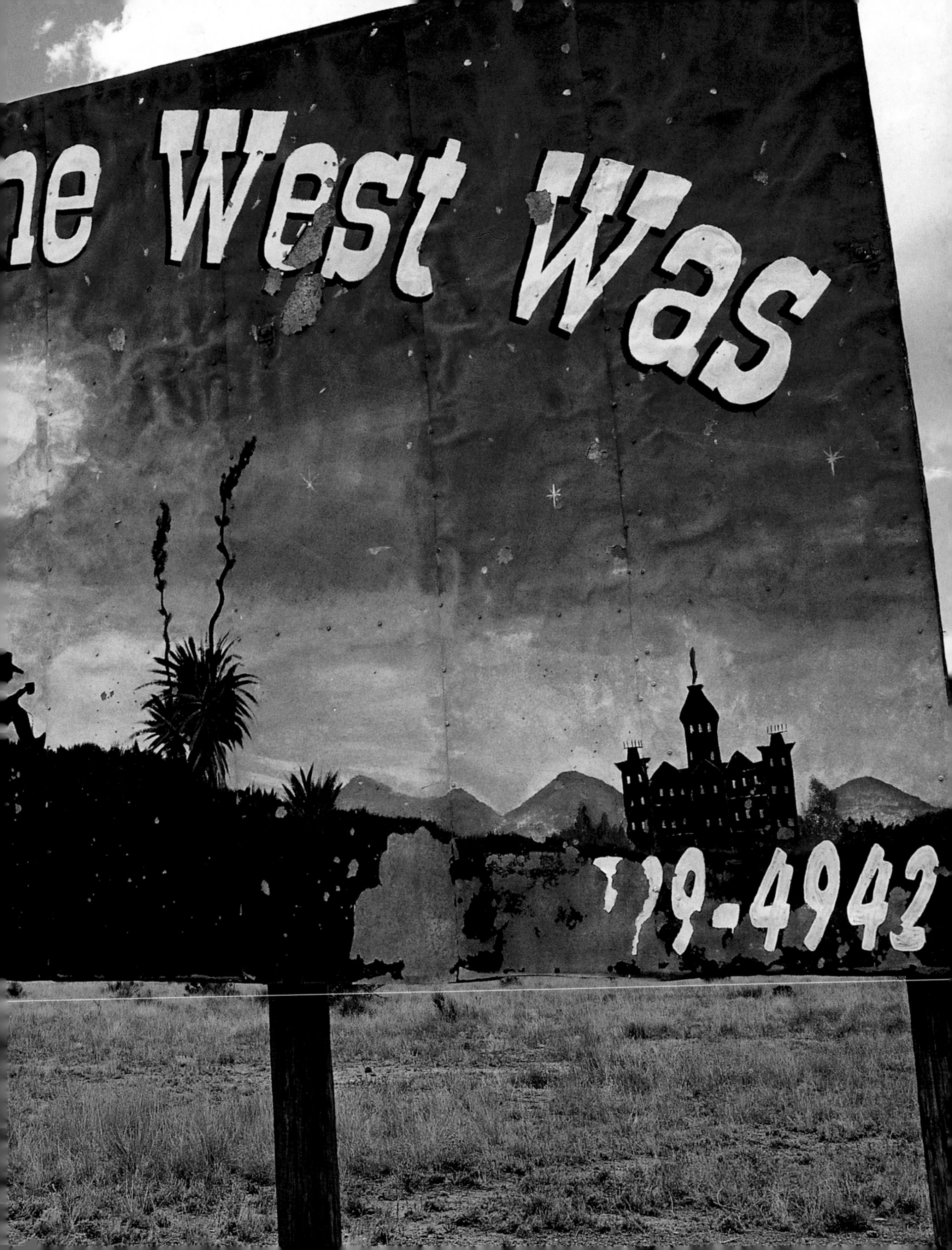
West Was
4942

Cowboy Minimalist

Until artist Donald Judd discovered this dusty but picturesque West Texas cowtown in the 1970s, Marfa's main attraction was the "Marfa Mystery Lights" an eerie, unexplained display of flashing lights that, if you were lucky, sometimes illuminated the town's inky-black star-filled sky after midnight. Nowadays, there is a lot more activity in Marfa, since Judd's famed Chinati Foundation draws art enthusiasts from all over the world to visit the installation of site-specific large-scale artworks on a former military base on Marfa's outskirts. The newcomers have brought their big-city culture to the small town, and nowadays Marfa is a place where you can, in the same day, drink a long-necked Budweiser with a guy in cowboy boots, and, eat grilled raddichio and gorgonzola appetizers with a New York art gallery manager. The Thunderbird Motel, on the surface, would seem to be a place that caters to the latter customer – it exudes the hip confidence of an owner who understands that old American 1950s motels are the quintessence of minimalist hip, especially when outfitted with fine cotton sheets from India, custom-built pecan-wood furniture, and Broadband internet connections. But the Thunderbird Motel, like the Chinati museum, is an upstart with a sense of place; it may bring new ideas to Marfa, but it embraces its surroundings and its West Texas roots. The motel's pale blue façade blends into the big sky of Texas; its jasmine-covered trellises are made from salvaged oil pipeline, and in the courtyard, there's a big slab of mesquite wood for a table. City slickers and cowboys should feel equally at home in this outpost of the new Marfa.

Book to Pack: "Complete Writings 1959-1975" by Donald Judd. Reviews, essays and criticism by the American artist and Chinati Foundation founder.

Thunderbird Motel
600 West San Antonio
Marfa, TX 79843
USA
Tel. +1 432 729 1984
Fax +1 432 729 1989
Email: reservations@thunderbirdmarfa.com
Website: www.thunderbirdmarfa.com
www.great-escapes-hotels.com

DIRECTIONS	On Highway 90, 190 miles (300 km) southeast of El Paso International Airport.
RATES	$
ROOMS	24 rooms, expanding to 40 by the end of 2006.
FOOD	Restaurant planned for 2006.
HISTORY	Renovated classic American motel, originally built 1959, opened 2005.
X-FACTOR	Cowboy minimalist motel from the proprietor of Austin's Hotel San José.

Minimalistisches Cowboy-Motel

Bevor der Künstler Donald Judd in den Siebzigern die zwar pittoreske, aber staubige Kleinstadt Marfa im Westen von Texas entdeckte, war hier nicht viel los. Als einzige Attraktion machten die »Marfa Mystery Lights« von sich reden, ein unerklärliches Phänomen, das sich nachts bei schwarzem, sternenbehangenem Himmel als strahlende, leuchtende Punkte am Horizont zeigt. Die öden Zeiten sind für Marfa ein für allemal vorbei. Judds Chinati Foundation lockt eine ganze Heerschar von Kunstfans aus aller Welt zu den riesigen, permanenten Installationen, die auf einer ehemaligen Militärbasis am Rande Marfas stehen. Der frische Wind hat etwas Großstadtkultur in die Kleinstadt gebracht, und heute kann man in Marfa mit einem Kerl in Cowboy-Boots ein Bier trinken und dann mit einem New Yorker Galeristen Raddichio mit Gorgonzola verspeisen. Das »Thunderbird Motel« wirkt auf den ersten Blick urban – eine Ikone des Minimalismus der Fünfziger Amerikas, kombiniert mit Baumwollwäsche aus Indien, handgefertigten Möbeln aus Pekanholz und Breitband-Internetanschluss. Doch das »Thunderbird Motel« hat, genau wie das »Chinati Museum«, seine texanischen Wurzeln nicht vergessen. Die hellblauen Fassaden des Motels und der weite Himmel von Texas fließen ineinander, der Jasmin wächst über ein Geflecht von alten Öl-Rohrleitungen und im Hinterhof wurde eine Mesquite-Holzplatte zu einem Tisch umfunktioniert. Hier fühlen sich Landeier genau so wohl wie Stadt-Cowboys.

Buchtipp: »Donald Judd« von Donald Judd und Nicholas Serota.
Würdigung des einflussreichen amerikanischen Künstlers und Gründer der Chinati Foundation in Marfa.

Western minimaliste

Jusqu'à ce que l'artiste Donald Judd découvre ce bourg poussiéreux mais pittoresque dans l'ouest du Texas dans les années soixante-dix, la principale attraction de Marfa était ses « lumières mystérieuses », des éclairs inexpliqués et inquiétants qui, parfois, illuminent le ciel étoilé après minuit. Il s'y passe beaucoup plus de choses depuis que la fondation « Chinati » ouverte par Judd attire des amateurs d'art venus des quatre coins du monde pour visiter l'installation de grandes œuvres contextuelles sur une ancienne base militaire à la lisière de Marfa. Les nouveaux venus ont importé leur culture métropolitaine et, dans la petite ville tranquille, on peut, dans la foulée, siroter une bière avec un cow-boy en santiags puis déguster des « raddichio et gorgonzolas grillés » avec un galeriste new-yorkais. En apparence, le « Thunderbird Motel » semble avoir été créé pour cette seconde catégorie de clients. Il dégage la suave assurance d'un propriétaire qui sait que les motels des années cinquante sont la quintessence du minimalisme branché, surtout équipés de draps en fin coton indien, de meubles sur-mesure en pacanier et de connexions Internet à haut débit. Mais, à l'instar du musée « Chinati », le motel est un lieu ambitieux qui sait s'intégrer. S'il apporte de nouvelles idées à Marfa, il a également fait siennes les racines de l'Ouest. Sa façade bleu pâle se fond dans le grand ciel texan, ses treillis couverts de jasmin sont faits de vieux pipelines et, dans la cour, une planche en proposis massif fait office de table. Citadins et cow-boys se sentent chez eux dans cet avant-poste de la Nouvelle Marfa.

Livre à emporter : « Écrits 1963-1990 » de Donald Judd.
Critiques et essais de l'artiste américain, créateur de la fondation Chinati.

ANREISE	300 km auf dem Highway 90 südöstlich vom internationalen Flughafen El Paso.	ACCÈS	Sur le Highway 90, à 300 km au sud-est de l'aéroport international d'El Paso.
PREISE	$	PRIX	$
ZIMMER	24 Zimmer. Bis Ende 2006 auf 40 Zimmer erweitert.	CHAMBRES	24 chambres, 40 à partir de fin 2006.
KÜCHE	Ein Restaurant ist für 2006 geplant.	RESTAURATION	Ouverture d'un restaurant prévue pour 2006.
GESCHICHTE	Renoviertes, klassisch amerikanisches Motel von 1959, 2005 wiedereröffnet.	HISTOIRE	Motel américain classique construit en 1959 et rénové en 2005.
X-FAKTOR	Minimalistisches »Cowboy-Motel«.	LE « PETIT PLUS »	« Motel cow-boy minimaliste », appartenant au même propriétaire que l'« Hotel San José » d'Austin.

Big Bend...
Cibolo Creek Ranch, Marfa

Big Bend

The legend is that the Cibolo Creek Ranch got its start as a getaway hideout. In the American West of the mid-1800s, gunfight duels were still more popular, and cheaper, than courts and lawyers for resolving disputes. But the duel winners usually had to run from justice, so after Milton Faver shot his rival, he quickly fled to the most remote and isolated place he could find, in order to start a new life. Today, Faver's old ranch – 32,000 acres straddling the Rio Grande river where it makes its "big bend" at the Texas-Mexico border – provides a different kind of refuge, an escape to the lost romance of the American West. It remains as remote as it was in the old wild West days (arrival here involves a three and a half hour drive or a private plane), but the working cattle ranch has been painstakingly restored as a luxury retreat. There are beautiful details here: Mexican carnival masks adorn the walls, original broad wooden beams secure the ceilings. Late at night, huddled under a colourful Southwestern blanket in your room in one of three historic adobe forts, you may hear wild boars rooting around in the sagebrush. Daylight activities at the ranch range from the old-fashioned to the modern. There are horses or 4-wheel drive vehicles to ride across the high mesas, a heated swimming pool and Jacuzzi to relax in. Or you can fast-forward to the ultra-contemporary, and drive a half hour north to visit Donald Judd's cool aluminium sculpture installations at the Chinati Foundation in Marfa. Being a fugitive from justice probably never was this much fun.

Book to pack: "Riders of the Purple Sage" by Zane Grey.
The early 20th century classic by the famous Western genre novelist.

Cibolo Creek Ranch
HCR 67, PO Box 44
Marfa, TX 79843
USA
Tel. +1 432 229 3737
Fax +1 432 229 3653
Email: reservations@cibolocreekranch.com
Website: www.cibolocreekranch.com
www.great-escapes-hotels.com

DIRECTIONS	The ranch is located a 225 miles (360 km) southwest of Midland (Texas) Airport, and 214 miles (340 km) southeast of El Paso (Texas) airport.
RATES	$$$
ROOMS	34 guest rooms in the fort buildings and guest house.
FOOD	Eclectic cuisine, using local ingredients like antelope and quail, and Mexican-Texas inspired dishes.
HISTORY	Cibolo's three historic frontier forts date back to the mid 19th Century. The property was restored and opened as a guest resort in 1994.
X-FACTOR	Luxurious and authentic immersion in the solitude and wilderness of the old Texas frontier.

Leben wie ein Cowboy

Im 18. Jahrhundert pflegte man im Westen Amerikas Streitereien nicht am Gericht zu regeln, sondern ganz unkompliziert mit einem Pistolen-Duell. Eine damals beliebte Methode und dazu noch kostengünstig. Wer aus einem solchen Duell als Sieger hervorkam, musste sich meist vor dem Gesetz verstecken. So etwa Milton Faver. Er streckte seinen Rivalen nieder und floh an den abgelegensten Ort, den er finden konnte, um dort ein neues Leben zu beginnen. Heute ist Favers 13 000 Hektar große »Cibolo Creek Ranch« entlang des Rio Grande an der texanisch-mexikanischen Grenze eine romantische Erinnerung an den Wilden Westen. Die Ranch liegt genauso abgeschieden wie damals und ist mit dem Auto von Midland oder El Paso in dreieinhalb Stunden zu erreichen, sonst nur mit einem Privatflugzeug. Auf der »Cibolo Creek Ranch« wird immer noch Viehzucht betrieben, auch wenn heute daraus ein sorgfältig umgebautes Luxus-Resort geworden ist. Ganz im traditionellen Ranch-Stil zieren Karnevalsmasken aus Mexiko die Wände und rustikale, breite Holzbalken stützen die Decken. Spät nachts kann man sogar draußen in der Wüste Wildschweine hören, während man in einem Zimmer der historischen Adobe-Forts unter einer Folklore-Bettdecke kuschelt. Bei Tage vertreibt man sich die Zeit mit einer Fahrt im traditionellen Vierspänner hoch auf den Tafelbergen. Oder man entspannt im geheizten Pool oder Jacuzzi. Ein Leckerbissen für Kulturfans liegt eine halbe Stunde weiter nördlich: Die Chinati Foundation in Marfa mit den spektakulären Aluminium-Skulpturen des Künstlers Donald Judd.

Buchtipp: »Desperados« von Zane Grey.
Klassischer Western-Roman aus dem frühen 20. Jahrhundert.

Le grand coude

La légende veut que le « Cibolo Creek Ranch » ait été la planque d'un hors-la-loi en cavale. Dans le Far West du milieu du 19e siècle, il était plus simple – et meilleur marché – de régler ses litiges par un duel au revolver qu'en recourant aux tribunaux. Le hic, c'était que le vainqueur avait ensuite la justice aux trousses. C'est ainsi qu'après avoir abattu son rival, Milton Faver se réfugia dans le lieu le plus perdu qu'il trouva afin d'y refaire sa vie. Aujourd'hui, son ranch – 13 000 hectares à cheval sur le Rio Grande là où il décrit un « grand coude » : à la frontière entre le Mexique et le Texas, offre un autre type d'évasion : une plongée dans l'atmosphère romantique de la conquête de l'Ouest. Le lieu est toujours aussi isolé (on y accède après trois heures et demie de route ou en avion privé), mais la ferme et ses enclos à bestiaux ont été restaurés et convertis en luxueux complexe hôtelier. Les détails ont été soignés : masques de carnaval mexicains aux murs, plafonds en poutres apparentes. Tard dans la nuit, blotti sous une couverture indienne dans votre chambre située dans une des trois bâtisses fortifiées en adobe, vous entendrez peut-être les cochons sauvages fouiller la terre sous les armoises. Le jour, les activités vont du traditionnel à l'avant-garde. On peut explorer les hautes mesas à cheval ou en quatre-quatre, se détendre dans la piscine chauffée et le jacuzzi ; ou encore se projeter en avant dans l'ultramoderne en allant voir les sculptures en aluminium de Donald Judd à la « Chinati Foundation » de Marfa. Jamais être en cavale n'aura été aussi plaisant.

Livre à emporter : « La Cabane perdue » de Louis L'Amour.
Un classique par un des plus grands auteurs de westerns adventures.

ANFAHRT	Die Ranch liegt 360 km südwestlich vom Flughafen in Midland, Texas, und 340 km südöstlich vom Flughafen in El Paso, Texas.
PREISE	$$$
ZIMMER	34 Gästezimmer verteilt auf drei Forts und ein Cottage.
KÜCHE	Vielseitige Küche mit lokalen Zutaten wie Antilope oder Wachtel; Tex-Mex-Gerichte.
GESCHICHTE	Drei historische Grenz-Forts aus der Mitte des 19. Jahrhunderts. 1994 Umbau und Eröffnung als Luxus-Resort.
X-FAKTOR	Eine geschichtsträchtige und luxuriöse Welt mitten in der wilden Einsamkeit des Grenzgebietes zu Mexiko.

ACCÈS	Le ranch est situé à 360 km au sud-ouest de l'aéroport de Midland (Texas), et à 340 km au sud-est de celui d'El Paso (Texas).
PRIX	$$$
CHAMBRES	34 chambres dans trois bâtiments fortifiés et un chalet.
RESTAURATION	Cuisine éclectique à base de produits locaux comme l'antilope et la caille, plus des plats tex-mex.
HISTOIRE	Les trois forts de « Cibolo Creek Ranch » gardaient la frontière au milieu du 19e siècle. La propriété a été restaurée et convertie en complexe hôtelier en 1994.
LE « PETIT PLUS »	Une immersion luxueuse et authentique dans la solitude et la nature sauvage du Texas.

Five Star Dharma...
El Monte Sagrado, Taos

Five Star Dharma

The 1960s are long gone, but its visionaries and healers and hippies can still be found living – indeed, thriving – in American outposts like Taos, New Mexico. Taos is mystic central, and mysticism, it seems, attracts prosperity. Taos today is one of the richest towns in the Southwest. It boasts of having more massage therapists per capita than any other place in the U.S. It's no surprise that Taos is also home to the only luxury resort spa constructed around a Navajo (Native American) Sacred Circle. El Monte Sagrado is the brainchild of Tom Worrell, a philanthropist cum environmentalist, whose dream was to construct an ecologically sound luxury retreat in the desert at the foot of the Sangre de Cristo mountains. There is no doubt that he has created a unique oasis; El Monte is a marvellous fantasy enclave of adobe buildings, pools and fountains that burble gently and constantly. But, fear not – everything at El Monte is designed to be 100% eco-sensitive: the water is constantly recycled by something called a "Living Machine", and it is purified with a non-chlorine substance. There is a Native American sweat lodge in the resort's spa, which aims to, according to Worrell, "help people identify their own self." The treatments include a "life reading" massage and an "Egyptian Anointing" which involves chakras and gemstones and hot oils. There's also an animal therapy session for those interested in learning to talk to their pets. "If something works," asks Worrell, "Why ask why?"

Book to Pack: "The Teachings of Don Juan" by Carlos Castaneda.
Words of wisdom from a Native American shaman. This book is the bible of the New Age movement.

El Monte Sagrado
317 Kit Carson Road
Taos, NM 87571
USA
Tel. +1 505 758 3502
Fax +1 505 737 2985
Email: info@elmontesagrado.com
Website: www.elmontesagrado.com
www.great-escapes-hotels.com

DIRECTIONS	9 miles (15 KM) northwest of Taos Municipal Airport.
RATES	$$$
ROOMS	36 suites and casitas (little houses).
FOOD	De La Tierra restaurant, serving organic gourmet dishes like "Yak Chili".
HISTORY	The resort was opened in 2003 by Tom Worrell, a maverick philanthropist and environmentalist.
X-FACTOR	Recharge your mystical and spiritual batteries in the southwest's most luxurious eco-resort.

Fünf-Sterne-Dharma

Die Sechziger sind längst vorbei, doch noch immer gibt es
Visionäre, Heiler und Hippies aus der Zeit. Eine Hochburg
dieser Zunft ist Taos in New Mexico. Taos ist ein Zentrum
für Esoterik und hat damit seinen Wohlstand begründet.
Die Stadt gehört zu den wohlhabendsten im Südwesten der
Vereinigten Staaten und brüstet sich gerne damit, die höchste Dichte an Masseuren im ganzen Land zu haben. Taos
kann auch mit dem einzigen Luxus-Spa aufwarten, das rund
um eine heilige Stätte der Navajo-Indianer gebaut wurde.
Der Gründer von »El Monte Sagrado«, der Philanthrop und
Umweltschützer Tom Worrell, hat hier seinen Traum von
einem ökologisch verträglichen Luxus-Retreat verwirklicht.
Mitten in der Wüste, am Fuße der »Sangre de Cristo
Mountains«, schuf er eine einzigartige Oase. »El Monte« ist
eine zauberhafte Traumwelt aus Lehmziegel-Häusern, Pools
und Brunnen, aus denen sanft das Wasser plätschert. Trotz
der Annehmlichkeiten ist hier alles hundertprozentig um-
weltverträglich: So wird das Wasser dauernd wiederaufberei-
tet und mit einer chlorfreien Substanz gereinigt. Im Spa gibt
es eine rituelle Indianer-Sauna, eine »Sweat Lodge« die,
gemäß Worrell, »helfen soll, sein Innerstes zu erkennen«.
Unter den Behandlungen findet man auch »Life-Reading«-
Massagen und »Egyptian Anointing«, eine ägyptische
Chakra-Ölung mit Edelsteinen und heißen Ölen. Auch
Haustierhalter kommen zum Zug: In einer speziellen
Therapiestunde lernt man, mit Tieren zu kommunzieren.
»Es funktioniert«, versichert Worrell.

Buchtipp: »Die Lehren des Don Juan« von Carlos Castaneda.
Weisheiten eines Indianer-Schamanen. Das Buch ist die
Bibel der New-Age-Bewegung.

Le dharma cinq étoiles

Les années soixante sont loin mais les visionnaires, guéris-
seurs et hippys continuent de s'épanouir dans des avant-
postes tels que Taos, au Nouveau-Mexique. Cette Mecque du
mysticisme doit attirer la prospérité car elle est aujourd'hui
l'une des agglomérations les plus riches du Sud-Ouest américain. Elle se targue de compter plus de massothérapeutes
par habitant que n'importe quelle autre ville des États-Unis.
Il n'y a donc rien d'étonnant à ce qu'elle abrite le seul spa de
grand standing construit autour d'un « cercle sacré » navajo.
« El Monte Sagrado » est l'œuvre de Tom Worrell, philan-
thrope et écologiste qui rêvait de bâtir une retraite de luxe
respectueuse de l'environnement dans le désert au pied du
massif de « Sangre de Cristo ». Il a su créer un lieu de rêve :
une merveilleuse oasis de bâtiments en adobe, de bassins et
de fontaines qui gargouillent doucement. Mais n'ayez crain-
te, tout à « El Monte » a été conçu dans le plus grand respect
de la nature : l'eau est recyclée en permanence par une
« machine vivante » et purifiée par une substance sans chlo-
re. Il y a une « hutte de sudation rituelle » qui, selon Worrell,
« aide chacun à identifier son moi ». Les traitements incluent
un « massage de lecture de vie » et des « onctions égyptien-
nes » qui font intervenir les chakras, des gemmes et des hui-
les chaudes. Il existe même des séances de thérapie animale
pour ceux qui souhaitent apprendre à communiquer avec
leurs matous et toutous chéris. « Si ça marche, il ne faut pas
chercher à savoir pourquoi », déclare Worrell.

**Livre à emporter : « Le Voyage à Ixtlan : les leçons de Don
Juan » de Carlos Castaneda.**
Des perles de sagesse offertes par un shaman amérindien.
Bible du mouvement New Age.

ANREISE	15 km nordwestlich vom Flughafen Taos.
PREISE	$$$
ZIMMER	36 Suiten und Casitas (kleine Häuser).
KÜCHE	Im Restaurant »De La Tierra« gibt's Bio-Gourmetgerichte wie »Yak Chili«.
GESCHICHTE	Das Resort wurde 2003 vom Philanthropen und Umweltschützer Tom Worrell gegründet.
X-FAKTOR	Auftanken in einem der luxuriösesten Öko-Resorts Amerikas.

ACCÈS	À 15 km au nord-ouest de l'aéroport municipal de Taos.
PRIX	$$$
CHAMBRES	36 suites et « casitas » (petites maisons).
RESTAURATION	Le restaurant « De La Tierra » sert des plats gastrono-miques bios tels que le « Chili au yack ».
HISTOIRE	L'hôtel a été ouvert en 2003 par Tom Worrell, un phi-lanthrope et écologiste anticonformiste.
LE « PETIT PLUS »	Rechargez vos batteries mystiques et spirituelles dans l'hôtel écologique le plus luxueux du Sud-Ouest.

Great Spirits...
The Mabel Dodge Luhan House, Taos

Great Spirits

The guest list of the Mabel Dodge Luhan house reads like an intellectual, cultural and artistic history of the twentieth century: Carl Jung, Willa Cather, Georgia O'Keeffe, Ansel Adams, Edmund Wilson, Aldous Huxley, Martha Graham. It was D.H. Lawrence who painted the vibrant red, yellow and blue stained glass windows that surround the bed in the main bedroom; Willa Cather, the well-known American novelist, came to Mabel Dodge Luhan's house to write. There are few places in America where a guest can sleep surrounded by so many great bohemian spirits of the past. Mabel Dodge Luhan, a socialite and patron of the arts from New York City's Greenwich Village, came to Taos in 1918, and soon afterwards married her fourth husband, Tony Luhan, a Pueblo Indian. Together they built this quirky adobe house full of windows to let in the brilliant blue light of the Taos, New Mexico sun. Their friends came, and stayed, and wrote, painted, and talked. That time has long passed, but something of that bright bohemian spirit remains in the sunsplashed spaces of this house, which is now open to guests as a bed and breakfast. Sit in a quiet corner by the window, and see if you can hear the whispers of dazzling conversations past.

Book to Pack: "The Rainbow" by D.H. Lawrence.
Novel by one of the Mabel Dodge Luhan house's most famous guests.

The Mabel Dodge Luhan House	
240 Morada Lane, PO Box 558	
Taos, NM 87571	
USA	
Tel. +1 505 751 9686	
Email: mabel@mabeldodgeluhan.com	
Website: www.mabeldodgeluhan.com	
www.great-escapes-hotels.com	

DIRECTIONS	9 miles (15 km) northwest of Taos Municipal Airport.
RATES	$
ROOMS	11 rooms.
FOOD	Breakfasts only, served in the original dining room.
HISTORY	Built by the bohemian "new woman" Mabel Dodge Luhan and her husband Tony in the 1920s, the house became a magnet for the great intellectuals and writers of the period.
X-FACTOR	Sleep in an architectural treasure of a house, filled with the spirits of extraordinary intellectuals and artists.

Berühmte Gäste

Die Gästeliste des »Mabel-Dodge-Luhan«-Hauses liest sich wie das »Who is Who« der Intelligenzija und Künstlerszene des zwanzigsten Jahrhunderts. Carl Jung war hier, Willa Cather, Georgia O'Keeffe, Ansel Adams, Edmund Wilson, Aldous Huxley und Martha Graham. D.H. Lawrence griff hier sogar zum Pinsel und malte die Fensterscheiben im großen Schlafzimmer knallrot, gelb und blau. Willa Cather, eine amerikanische Romanautorin, reiste ins Haus von Mabel Dodge Luhan, um zu schreiben. Es gibt nur wenige Orte in Amerika, die von so viel Künstlergeist beseelt sind. Mabel Dodge Luhan, Dame der Gesellschaft und Kunst-mäzenin aus Greenwich Village in New York, kam 1918 nach Taos, New Mexico, und heiratete kurz nach ihrer Ankunft Ehemann Nummer Vier, Tony Luhan, einen Pueblo-Indianer. Zusammen bauten sie ein eigenwilliges Lehmziegel-Haus mit vielen Fenstern, durch die das strahlend blaue Licht von Taos hineinströmt. Oft kamen Freunde des Paares zu Besuch, schrieben, malten und diskutierten. Das ist zwar längst Vergangenheit, doch noch immer schwebt etwas von diesem Künstlergeist durch die sonnendurchfluteten Räume des heutigen »Bed and Breakfast«. Und schaut man zum Fenster hinaus, kann man wunderbar von vergangenen Zeiten träumen.

Buchtipp: »Der Regenbogen« von D.H. Lawrence.
Novelle von einem der berühmtesten Gästen vom »Mabel-Dodge-Luhan«-Haus.

Les grands esprits

La liste des hôtes de la « Mabel Dodge Luhan House » ressemble à une histoire intellectuelle, culturelle et artistique du 20e siècle : Carl Jung, Willa Cather, Georgia O'Keeffe, Ansel Adams, Edmund Wilson, Aldous Huxley, Martha Graham. Les vitraux rouges, jaunes et bleus qui entourent le lit dans la chambre principale furent réalisés par D. H. Lawrence. La célèbre romancière américaine Willa Cather vint s'y installer pour écrire. Il existe peu d'endroits aux États-Unis où l'on peut s'endormir bercé par les fantômes de tant de grands esprits bohèmes du passé. La New-Yorkaise Mabel Dodge, grande mondaine et mécène, quitta le Greenwich Village pour s'installer à Taos en 1918 où elle rencontra peu après son quatrième mari, Tony Luhan, un Indien Pueblo. Ensemble, ils construisirent cette demeure excentrique en adobe pleine de fenêtres pour laisser entrer le soleil du Nouveau-Mexique. Leurs amis vinrent et restèrent, écrivant, peignant, discutant. Cette époque est loin maintenant mais il subsiste quelque chose de cette ambiance inspirée et bohème dans ces espaces inondés d'une belle lumière bleutée. La maison est désormais convertie en maison d'hôtes. Asseyez-vous dans un petit coin tranquille près d'une fenêtre et essayez d'entendre le murmure des conversations brillantes du passé.

Livre à emporter : « L'Arc-en-ciel » de D.H. Lawrence.
Roman de l'un des invités les plus célèbres de « Mabel Dodge Luhan House ».

ANREISE	15 km nordwestlich vom Flughafen Taos.
PREISE	$
ZIMMER	11 Zimmer.
KÜCHE	Nur Frühstück im Speisezimmer.
GESCHICHTE	Das Haus der unkonventionellen Mabel Dodge Luhan und ihrem Mann Tony aus den 1920er Jahren war Anziehungspunkt für die großen Intellektuellen und Schriftsteller der Zeit.
X-FAKTOR	Außergewöhnliche Architektur erfüllt von dem Geist und Animus Intellektueller und Künstler.

ACCÈS	15 km au nord-ouest de l'aéroport municipal de Taos.
PRIX	$
CHAMBRES	11 chambres.
RESTAURATION	Petits-déjeuners uniquement, servis dans la salle à manger qui a conservé son décor original.
HISTOIRE	Construite par la « nouvelle femme » bohème Mabel Dodge Luhan et son mari Tony dans les années vingt, la maison devint un lieu de rencontre des grands intellectuels et écrivains de l'époque.
LE « PETIT PLUS »	Dormez dans un trésor architectural, une demeure peuplée par les fantômes d'intellectuels et d'artistes extraordinaires.

Up to Your Neck...
Ten Thousand Waves, Sante Fe

Ten Thousand Waves, Sante Fe

Up to Your Neck

There's an argument to be made that water-specifically mineral-rich spring water that bubbles naturally from deep inside the earth-is the most potent drug on the planet. It is an argument that seems especially compelling after about twenty minutes soaking in a deep tub of intensely hot, steaming water. The Japanese understand the power of water, and they have created a whole culture around the act of hot springs bathing, and raised it to an aesthetic experience. Few places in the U.S. understand the subtleties of the Japanese bath, but at Ten Thousand Waves the onsen culture has been transplanted almost intact from the Japanese woods to the American high desert. The centrepieces of Ten Thousand Waves, as in Japan, are the two outdoor communal tubs, or "ofuro". One is for both sexes, the other for women only, and both are built in harmony with the outdoors; tiny rock gardens hold small iron lanterns, the railings are rough-hewn timbers, and bathing areas are separated by traditional Shoji screens. Ten Thousand Waves was originally a hot springs spa for day guests, but some years ago the owners decided to add some suites so that the completely unwound and de-stressed customers wouldn't have to worry about finding their way home after the bath. The suites are decorated in the same satisfyingly rustic Southwest-meets-Mt. Fuji style as the pool areas. Slip into the hot water on a cool, dry desert night, lean back, look up, and wonder: Do the stars shine so brightly in Tokyo?

Book to pack: "Memoirs of a Geisha" by Arthur Golden
Historical novel about Japanese geishas and their lifestyle.

Ten Thousand Waves	
3451 Hyde Park Road	
Santa Fe, NM 87504	
USA	
Tel. +1 505 992 5052	
Website: www.tenthousandwaves.com	
www.great-escapes-hotels.com	

DIRECTIONS	3.5 miles (5 km) west of Santa Fe.
RATES	$$
ROOMS	12 guest suites.
FOOD	No food; some guest suites have hibachi grills.
HISTORY	Originally only a hot tub spa retreat; guest suites were added in 1997.
X-FACTOR	For authentic Japanese hot springs bathing under the New Mexico desert sky.

Einfach eintauchen und entspannen

Wasser ist eines der wirksamsten Heilmittel überhaupt. Erst
recht, wenn es reich an Mineralien ist und aus einer Quelle
aus dem tiefen Inneren der Erde sprudelt. Nach zwanzig
Minuten in der heiß-dampfenden Wanne fängt man an, die
Wohltaten zu spüren. Die Japaner haben eine ganze Kultur
rund ums heiße Bad entwickelt und sie zum ästhetischen
Erlebnis erhoben. Nur wenige Spas in den Vereinigten
Staaten verstehen die Feinheiten der japanischen Badekul-
tur. Zu den Ausnahmen gehört »Ten Thousand Waves«, ein
Spa, das die Rituale des heißen Quellbades in die Wüste
New Mexicos gebracht hat. Zwei gemeinschaftlich genutzte
»Ofuro«-Becken (das eine für Frauen und Männer, das andere nur für Frauen) bilden nach japanischem Vorbild das
Herzstück. Sie liegen harmonisch in der freien Natur. Mi-
niatur-Steingärten verankern kleine Eisenlaternen, die Ge-
länder sind aus grob gehobelten Holzbalken gezimmert, und
die Badezonen sind mit traditionellen »Shoji«-Wandschir-
men abgetrennt. »Ten Thousand Waves« war zunächst aus-
schließlich als Spa konzipiert. Damit die Gäste nach dem
Bad nicht aus ihrer wohligen Entspannung herausgerissen
werden, haben die Besitzer vor ein paar Jahren Suiten hin-
zugebaut. Sie sind im ansprechenden Dekor des Spas gehal-
ten - ein Mix aus rustikalem Western-Stil und Fuji-Ästhetik.
Am schönsten ist ein nächtliches Bad unter klarem Sternen-
himmel. Denn nirgendwo strahlen die Sterne so hell wie
hier.

Buchtipp: »Die Geisha« von Arthur Golden
Historischer Roman über das Leben der Geishas in Japan.

Jusqu'au cou

D'aucuns soutiennent que l'eau de source riche en sels
minéraux qui jaillit directement des entrailles de la terre est
la drogue la plus puissante de la planète. On est tenté de le
croire après avoir trempé vingt minutes dans une profonde
cuve fumante. Les Japonais comprennent le pouvoir de l'eau
au point d'avoir créé toute une culture autour du bain dans
des sources chaudes, l'érigeant en expérience esthétique.
Peu d'endroits aux États-Unis comprennent les subtilités du
bain japonais mais, à « Ten Thousand Waves », la tradition
« onsen » des forêts du Japon a été transplantée quasi intacte
dans le haut désert américain. Ici, les pièces maîtresses sont
les deux « ofuro », des bassins collectifs en plein air. L'un est
mixte, l'autre réservé aux femmes et tous deux s'harmoni-
sent avec la nature. De minuscules jardins de pierres sont
éclairés par de petites lanternes en fer, les balustrades sont
en bois brut et les bains sont séparés par des écrans traditionnels « Shoji ». À l'origine, « Ten Thousand Waves » n'ac-
cueillait les thermalistes que pendant la journée, jusqu'à ce
que les propriétaires n'ajoutent quelques suites pour que
leurs clients complètement relaxés n'aient pas à s'inquiéter
de devoir reprendre la route. Le décor des chambres témoig-
ne du même mariage heureux entre l'ouest américain et le
style du mont Fuji que les thermes. Glissez-vous lentement
dans l'eau chaude par une fraîche nuit dans le désert, détendez-vous et admirez le ciel : les étoiles ont-elles autant d'é-
clat à Tokyo ?

Livre à emporter : « Geisha » de Arthur Golden
Roman historique sur la vie des geishas japonaises.

ANREISE	5 km westlich von Santa Fe.
PREISE	$$
ZIMMER	12 Gästesuiten.
KÜCHE	Keine Verpflegungsmöglichkeiten. In einigen Suiten steht ein »Hibachi«-Grill.
GESCHICHTE	Ursprünglich nur ein Spa; Gästesuiten wurden 1997 dazugebaut.
X-FAKTOR	Authentische Badekultur aus Japan unter dem Wüsten-Himmel New Mexicos.

ACCÈS	5 km à l'ouest de Santa Fe.
PRIX	$$
CHAMBRES	12 suites.
RESTAURATION	Pas de restaurant ; certaines suites sont équipées de grills hibachi.
HISTOIRE	Initialement un spa de sources chaudes auquel des suites ont été ajoutées en 1997.
LE « PETIT PLUS »	Des bains de sources chaudes à la japonaise en plein air dans le désert du Nouveau Mexique.

Wild West Rocks...
Hotel Congress, Tucson

Wild West Rocks

"Everybody, eventually, ends up at the Hotel Congress," proclaims a Tucson lifestyle magazine. "Everybody", in this case, is the crème de la crème of this desert city's bohemian scene, from college students, to poets, to musicians. In the lower part of the hotel, there's a well-known rock and roll venue, Club Congress. The hotel's 40 rooms – iron bedsteads, ceiling fans – are conveniently located upstairs, above the hotel bars and the club, so you don't have to worry about how you're getting home from the party. Though it has a young, hipster feel, the Hotel Congress is rich in history, atmosphere, and ghosts. It was built in 1919, to cater to the railroad and cattle ranchers who made this southern Arizona town near the Mexican border boom at the turn of the 19th century. The lobby, with velvet curtains, leather chairs, and glass-windowed doors, looks straight out of a Wild West movie, or a Bob Dylan ballad. When the famous bank robber John Dillinger was running away from the police in 1934, he picked the Hotel Congress to hide out in. He stayed for a couple of weeks, then he got caught. But you don't have to be.

Book to pack: "The Dillinger Days" by John Toland.
Another American criminal case turned into a happy legend. History told like a story.

Hotel Congress	
311 East Congress Street	
Tucson, AZ 85701	
USA	
Tel. +1 520 622 8848	
Fax: +1 520 792 6366	
Email: reservations@hotelcongress.com	
Website: www.hotelcongress.com	
www.great-escapes-hotels.com	

DIRECTIONS	Located in downtown Tucson, Arizona about 7.5 miles (12 km) north of Tucson International Airport.
RATES	$
ROOMS	40 rooms, with double or twin beds. A few of the rooms have bunk beds and are shared, youth hostel style.
FOOD	The Cup Café serves breakfast, lunch and dinner – dishes from Indian to French. The Tap Room is the original hotel bar.
HISTORY	Built in 1919 when Tucson was still a small railroad and cattle town at the edge of America's wild West. The hotel was gangster John Dillinger's hideout in 1934.
X-FACTOR	Rock and roll hipsters meet outlaw chic.

Rock'n'Roll im Wilden Westen

In Tucson, Arizona, kommt kein Hippie um das »Hotel Congress« herum. Hier verkehren College-Studenten, Poeten und Musiker. Kurz, die ganze junge Szene der Wüstenstadt. Anziehungspunkt ist der »Club Congress« im Erdgeschoss des Hotels, der sich als der Ort für Rock'n'Roll weitum einen Namen gemacht hat. Für Hotelgäste ist dieser Umstand sehr praktisch: Nach der Party müssen sie nur schnell die Treppe hochklettern – und schon sind sie in ihren Betten. Ihnen stehen im ersten Stockwerk, direkt über dem Club und der Bar, 40 Zimmer mit altmodischen Eisenbetten und Deckenventilatoren zur Verfügung. Das »Hotel Congress« ist seit 1919 Teil der Stadtgeschichte. An der Wende vom 19. zum 20. Jahrhundert herrschte in Tucson Aufbruchstimmung: Eisenbahnbau und Viehzucht verhalfen der Stadt im Süden Arizonas zu ihrer Blüte. Der Geist längst vergangener Zeiten ist im »Congress« überall zu spüren. Samtvorhänge, verglaste Türen und Ledersessel in der Lobby erinnern an alte Western-Filme. Auch Bob Dylan würde ganz gut hierher passen. Und selbstverständlich kann das Hotel, wie es sich für den Wilden Westen gehört, mit einer ordentlichen Räubergeschichte aufwarten. 1934 versteckte sich hier der berüchtigte Bankräuber John Dillinger mit seiner Gang wochenlang vor der Polizei und wurde dann erwischt.

Buchtipp: »The Dillinger Days« von John Toland.
Und wieder ein amerikanischer Krimineller, der zur Legende geworden ist. Geschichte im Krimi-Format.

Les rockeurs de l'Ouest

« Tout le monde, un jour ou l'autre, atterrit à l'hôtel Congress », proclame un magazine de Tucson. « Tout le monde », en l'occurrence, c'est la crème des cercles bohèmes de cette ville du désert : étudiants, poètes ou musiciens. Le rez-de-chaussée abrite un club célèbre, le « Club Congress », on l'on écoute du rock. Les 40 chambres (lits en fer forgé, ventilateurs de plafond) se trouvent à l'étage, au-dessus des bars et du club de l'hôtel, si bien que « boire ou conduire » n'est plus un choix cornélien. En dépit de son ambiance jeune et branchée, l'« Hotel Congress » a une histoire riche chargée de fantômes. Il a été construit en 1919 pour accueillir les voyageurs du nouveau chemin de fer et les éleveurs de bétail à l'époque où cette ville du sud de l'Arizona proche de la frontière mexicaine était en plein essor. Le hall, avec ses rideaux en velours, ses fauteuils en cuir et ses portes vitrées, semble tout droit sorti d'un western ou d'une ballade de Bob Dylan. En 1934, John Dillinger, le célèbre braqueur de banques, vint s'y planquer. Il y séjourna plusieurs semaines avant de se laisser piéger. Mais vous n'êtes pas obligé d'en faire autant.

Livre à emporter : « Dillinger » de John Toland.
Encore une affaire criminelle américaine transformée en légende positive. Se lit comme un roman.

ANREISE	Im Zentrum der Stadt, etwa 12 km nördlich vom internationalen Flughafen Tucson, Arizona.
PREISE	$
ZIMMER	40 Zimmer, meist mit Einzel- oder Doppelbetten. Ein paar Zimmer haben Etagenbetten.
KÜCHE	Frühstück, Mittag- und Abendessen im »Cup Café«. Verschiedene Gerichte aus Indien, Amerika und Frankreich. Nicht verpassen: Ein Drink im »Tap Room«.
GESCHICHTE	Erbaut 1919, als Tucson noch eine kleine Eisenbahn-Stadt mitten im Wildem Westen war. 1934 diente dem landesweit bekannten Gangster John Dillinger als Versteck.
X-FAKTOR	Unkonventioneller Rock'n'Roll-Schick.

ACCÈS	Situé au centre de Tucson, dans l'Arizona, à environ 12 km au nord de l'aéroport international de Tucson.
PRIX	$
CHAMBRES	40 chambres, certaines avec un grand lit, d'autres des lits jumeaux. Plusieurs chambres ont des lits superposés.
RESTAURATION	Le « Cup Café » sert le petit-déjeuner, le déjeuner et le dîner. Jouez des coudes jusqu'au comptoir de la « Tap Room », le vieux bar de l'hôtel.
HISTOIRE	Construit en 1919. Le fameux bandit John Dillinger s'y réfugia avec son gang en 1934.
LE « PETIT PLUS »	La « rock'n'roll » attitude rencontre le chic canaille.

Mi Adobe Hacienda...
Rancho de la Osa, Tucson

Mi Adobe Hacienda

We are in the United States, but not quite. Once upon a time, this piece of beautiful high desert land in southern Arizona, where Rancho de la Osa sits, was part of Mexico. Before that it belonged to Spain, and still before that, the Navajo Indians made this place their home. Like all border-lands, the rugged valley between the Baboquivari peak and the Sierra Mountains retains an unexpected mix of cultures and folkways. You can taste them in the Rancho's daily menu, where ancient ingredients like Navajo corn and beans blend with Latin spices and servings of succulent meat (the big business here, until recently, was cattle ranching) roasted on mesquite wood chips. Rancho de la Osa is a place to immerse yourself in this unique American borderland culture; here, you can wander among old adobe buildings, sit under shady eucalyptus trees, listen to the gentle sounds of ranch life: the ring of the mission bell, voices chattering in both English and Spanish, the hoofbeats of horses. The horses, of course, are one of the Rancho's biggest attractions – it is a working dude ranch, where horses have been raised and trained for more than 300 years (In the 1920s and 1930s, Western movies were shot here, and the singing cowboy Tom Mix was a regular guest). There's a staff of vaqueros – that's cowboys to you – who will help you saddle up and ride into the surrounding grasslands and hills (the room rate includes two rides a day). If you are not a seasoned cowboy, at Rancho you can take riding lessons, and you can even borrow cowboy boots ("Shake them out before using," warns the Rancho guest manual.) Good advice, in any language.

Book to pack: "The Milagro Beanfield War" by John Nichols.
Novel about the history of the American-Mexican border-lands; made into a Robert Redford movie.

Rancho de la Osa	
P.O. Box 1	
Tucson/Sasabe, AZ 85633	
USA	
Tel. +1 520 823 4257	
Fax +1 520 823 4238	
Email: osagal@aol.com	
Website: www.ranchodelaosa.com	
www.great-escapes-hotels.com	

DIRECTIONS	Located about 92 miles (150 km) southwest of the Tucson, Arizona airport.
RATES	$$
ROOMS	19 mountain-view guest rooms, most with fireplaces; each one is different and filled with Mexican antiques.
FOOD	Modern Southwestern American-style meals – tortilla soup, mesquite grilled meats – are served in the ochre-walled dining room in the main hacienda building.
HISTORY	The ranch is more than three hundred years old, and dates back to the time of the Spanish missions.
X-FACTOR	Stunning desert nights, old Spanish Southwest culture.

Fiesta Mexicana

Die Heimat der »Rancho de la Osa« im Süden Arizonas ist anders als der Rest der Vereinigten Staaten. Kein Wunder: Das Gebiet gehörte einst zu Mexiko und zuvor der spanischen Krone. Bevor die Kolonialmacht Besitzansprüche stellte, hatten hier allerdings die Navajo-Indianer das Sagen. Im rauen Tal zwischen dem »Baboquivari Peak« und den »Sierra Mountains« vermischen sich Kulturen und Traditionen. In der Küche werden zum Beispiel traditionelle Zutaten wie Navajo-Mais und Bohnen genauso verwendet wie lateinamerikanische Gewürze. Eine Spezialität ist Kakteenfleisch, das über dem wohlriechendem Mesquite-Holz gebraten wird, und der Anbau und Handel von Kakteen hat sich hier zu einem blühenden Geschäft entwickelt. Wer die amerikanisch-mexikanische Grenzkultur erleben möchte, ist auf der »Rancho de la Osa« genau richtig. Hier kann man an traditonellen Lehmziegel-Häusern vorbeispazieren, unter schattigen Eukalyptusbäumen sitzen und dabei dem Leben auf der Ranch zuhören: hier das Läuten einer alten Kirchenglocke, da ein Stimmengewirr zwischen Englisch und Spanisch und dort Pferdehufschlag. Seit über 300 Jahren werden hier Pferde gezüchtet und trainiert, und trotz Gästen wird noch richtig gearbeitet. In den Zwanzigern und Dreißigern wurden hier auch einige Western-Filme gedreht. Die Pferde sind die größte Attraktion der Ranch. Die Vaqueros, der spanische Ausdruck für Cowboys, helfen den Gästen gerne für den Ausritt in den Sattel. Ein erfahrener Reiter braucht man allerdings nicht zu sein – es gibt Reitstunden. Und die passenden Cowboy-Boots kann man sich dazu auch noch ausleihen.

Buchtipp: »Milagro« von John Nichols.

Das Buch zum Film von Robert Redford. Eine Geschichte aus dem amerikanisch-mexikanischen Grenzgebiet.

Mon hacienda en adobe

On est aux États-Unis mais pas tout à fait. Autrefois, cette partie du désert au sud de l'Arizona était mexicaine. Avant cela, elle fut espagnole et, plus loin encore, terre des Navajos. Comme toutes les régions frontalières, cette vallée sauvage blottie entre le pic « Baboquivari » et la « Sierra Mountains » abrite un surprenant mélange de cultures et de coutumes. On le sent dans la cuisine du Rancho, où des ingrédients comme le maïs et les haricots navajos s'associent aux épices latino-américaines pour accompagner les viandes succulentes (jusqu'à récemment, l'élevage était l'activité principale du ranch) grillées sur des copeaux de prosopis. « Le Rancho de la Osa » est le lieu rêvé pour baigner dans cette ambiance unique. Promenez-vous parmi les vieilles bâtisses en adobe, asseyez-vous à l'ombre des eucalyptus, laissez-vous bercer par les bruits familiers : la cloche de la mission, les bribes de conversation en anglais et en espagnol, le martèlement des sabots de chevaux. Ces derniers, naturellement, sont la grande attraction de l'établissement, qui les dresse depuis plus de 300 ans (dans les années vingt et trente, on tournait ici des westerns, et le cow-boy chanteur Tom Mix était un habitué). Une équipe de « vaqueros » vous aidera à grimper en selle pour un galop dans les prairies et les collines environnantes (le prix de la chambre inclut deux balades par jour). Si vous n'êtes pas un cavalier chevronné, le Rancho offre des cours. Vous pouvez même emprunter des bottes de cow-boy (le guide du Rancho met en garde « Secouez-les bien avant de les enfiler. » Un bon conseil, dans toutes les langues).

Livre à emporter : « Milagro ou la guerre des haricots » de John Nichols.

Roman sur l'histoire de la frontière américano-mexicaine, adapté à l'écran par Robert Redford.

ANREISE	Etwa 150 km südwestlich vom Flughafen Tucson, Arizona.
PREISE	$$
ZIMMER	19 Zimmer mit Sicht auf die Berge, die meisten mit Kamin, und alle mit mexikanischen Antiquitäten eingerichtet.
KÜCHE	Spezialitäten des amerikanischen Südwestens wie Tortillasuppe oder Grilladen auf Mesquite-Holz werden im ockerfarbenen Speisesaal der Hacienda serviert.
GESCHICHTE	Die Ranch wurde vor mehr als 300 Jahren während der spanischen Kolonialzeit gegründet.
X-FAKTOR	Atemberaubend schöne Wüstennächte; amerikanisch-mexikanische Kultur des Südwestens.

ACCÈS	Situé à 150 km au sud-ouest de l'aéroport de Tucson, dans l'Arizona.
PRIX	$$
CHAMBRES	19 chambres avec vue sur la montagne, la plupart avec cheminée.
RESTAURATION	Cuisine américaine moderne typique du Sud-Ouest. Les repas sont servis dans la salle à manger ocre dans le bâtiment principal de l'hacienda.
HISTOIRE	Vieux de plus de 300 ans, le ranch date de l'époque des missions espagnoles.
LE « PETIT PLUS »	Nuits somptueuses sous le ciel du désert.

DING

ARLENE'S

AR

Silver Boxes...

Shady Dell RV Park, Bisbee

Silver Boxes

In the 1950s, decades before Motel 6 and Days Inns turned America's budget motels into a standardized, fast-food experience, this is how Americans travelled on the cheap. Families packed up and headed out on the highway in a car with a silver box trailing behind it. These yachts of the road had evocative names – Airstream, Manor, Royal Mansion – and sleek, aerodynamic shapes that hinted speed, open spaces, and freedom. The tourism slogan of the period was "See America First", and there probably never was a time when travelling overland across America's deserts and farmlands was more carefree or romantic. The Shady Dell RV Park is a tiny enclave that preserves 1950s trailer travelling in all its glory for contemporary travellers. Situated behind a gas station and next to a cemetery, about a mile away from the famous "Ghost Town" of Bisbee, Arizona, the trailer park is home to 10 vintage aluminium trailers and one beached wooden yacht that have been painstakingly restored into 1950s time capsules, down to the tiniest detail. Bedspreads are chenille, phonographs come with Elvis Presley 45rpm discs, and the cupboards hold antique Martini glasses and shakers. You can sip your Martini while staring out at the desert, then take a drive into nearby Bisbee, an abandoned copper mining town that's found a second life as a community for hippies, artisans and bohemians of all types. Or you can escape across the Mexican border, just a few miles down the highway. From inside a shiny silver box with wheels, anything and everything seems possible.

Book to pack: "Airstream, The History of the Land Yacht" by Bryan Burkhart and David Hunt.
An illustrated cultural history of American vintage trailers.

Shady Dell RV Park
1 Old Douglas Road
Bisbee, AZ 85603
USA
Tel. +1 520 432 3567
Email: reservations@theshadydell.com
Website: www.theshadydell.com
www.great-escapes-hotels.com

DIRECTIONS	Located about 92 miles (150 km) southeast of the Tucson, Arizona airport.
RATES	$
ROOMS	Ten vintage aluminium travel trailers from the 1940s and 1950s, and one beached Chris Craft Yacht.
FOOD	Dot's Diner, a 10-stool American diner, serves breakfasts and lunches between 7am and 2pm, Wednesday to Sunday.
HISTORY	An American roadside trailer park, opened in 1927, restored and re-fitted with vintage aluminum trailers in 1995 by a couple of former antique dealers.
X-FACTOR	The freedom and romance of Roadside America, circa 1950.

Silberne Schmuckkästchen

Im Amerika der fünfziger Jahre hatten Budget-Unterkünfte noch Stil. Billighotel-Ketten wie »Motel 9« oder »Days Inns« – mit dem Charme von Fast-Food-Restaurants – existierten noch nicht. Die typische amerikanische Familie packte ganz einfach ihre Siebensachen ins Auto und fuhr los. Hinten angehängt glitzerte ein silberner Wohnwagen. Es waren richtige Straßen-Yachten mit aerodynamischen Formen und so klingenden Namen wie »Airstream«, »Manor« oder »Royal Mansion«. Sie evozierten Träume von Geschwindigkeit, unendlich weiten Landschaften und der großen Freiheit. Nie war das Reisen quer durch Amerikas Wüsten und Felder unbeschwerter und romantischer. Der »Shady Dell RV (Recreational Vehicle) Park« hat ein Stück dieser gloriosen Fünfziger-Trailer-Romantik bewahrt. Er liegt keine zwei Kilometer außerhalb der Geisterstadt Bisbee in Arizona, gleich hinter einer Tankstelle und neben einem Friedhof. Zehn Wohnwagen aus Aluminium und eine gestrandete Holz-Yacht wurden bis ins letzte Detail restauriert und stehen hier als Zeitinsel der Fünfziger. Bettdecken aus Chenille, Elvis-Presley-Vinylplatten und klassische Martini-Gläser und -Shaker ergänzen das Stilbild stimmig. Mit dem Martini-Glas an den Lippen lässt sich der Blick auf die Wüstenlandschaft besonders gut genießen. Unbedingt empfiehlt sich ein Ausflug nach Bisbee, einer verlassenen Kupferminen-Stadt, die heute als Kommune für Hippies, Künstler und Bohemiens eine Renaissance erlebt. Oder man fährt kurz ein paar Meilen auf dem Highway über die Grenze nach Mexiko. Hat man eine glänzende Silber-Box auf Rädern als Zufluchtsort, scheint plötzlich alles möglich.

Buchtipp: »Airsteam, The History of the Land Yacht« von Bryan Burkhart und David Hunt.
Illustrierte Kulturgeschichte amerikanischer Trailer.

Des écrins d'argent

Dans les années cinquante, bien avant que des chaînes telles que « Motel 9 » et « Days Inn » ne transforment les motels bon marché américains en produits standardisés et aseptisés, c'est ainsi que les Américains voyageaient à peu de frais. Les familles prenaient la route avec la caravane accrochée à l'arrière de la voiture. Ces yachts sur roues aux noms suggestifs – « Airstream », « Manor », « Royal Mansion » – avaient des lignes aérodynamiques symboles de vitesse, de grands espaces et de liberté. La devise de l'époque était « voir l'Amérique d'abord ». Jamais voyager à travers les déserts et les champs des États-Unis n'avait fleuré aussi bon l'insouciance et le romantisme. Le « Shady Dell RV Park » est une minuscule enclave qui préserve ces joyaux pour le plus grand bonheur des voyageurs d'aujourd'hui. Situé entre une pompe à essence et un cimetière, à moins de deux kilomètres de la « ville fantôme » de Bisbee, en Arizona, il accueille dix caravanes en aluminium et un yacht en bois à sec, tous des années cinquante et minutieusement restaurés jusque dans leurs moindres détails : couvre-lits en chenille, phonographes équipés de vieux vinyles d'Elvis Presley, verres à martini et shakers d'époque. Vous pouvez sirotez votre cocktail tout en admirant le désert, puis faire un saut à Bisbee, qui, une fois les mines de cuivre désertées, est devenue une communauté de hippys, d'artisans et de marginaux de tous poils. Vous pouvez aussi fuir au Mexique, dont la frontière se trouve à deux pas. Douillettement blotti à l'intérieur d'un étincelant écrin d'argent monté sur roues, tout paraît possible.

Livre à emporter : « Airstream, The History of the Land Yacht » de Bryan Burkhart et David Hunt.
Une histoire illustrée de la culture de la caravane aux États-Unis.

ANREISE	Rund 150 km südöstlich vom Flughafen in Tucson, Arizona.
PREISE	$
ZIMMER	Zehn »Vintage-Aluminium-Wohnwagen« aus den 1940ern und 1950ern und eine gestrandete »Chris Craft Yacht«.
KÜCHE	»Dot's Diner«, ein typisch amerikanischer Diner mit zehn Plätzen, für Frühstück und Mittagessen, Mittwoch bis Sonntag zwischen 7 und 15 Uhr geöffnet.
GESCHICHTE	Amerikanischer Trailerpark aus dem Jahr 1927 von einem ehemaligen Antiquitätenhändler-Paar 1995 restauriert und mit Vintage-Aluminium-Wohnwagen bestückt.
X-FAKTOR	Freiheit und Romantik im Amerika der Fünfziger Jahre.

ACCÈS	Situé à environ 150 km au sud-est de l'aéroport de Tucson, dans l'Arizona.
PRIX	$
CHAMBRES	Dix caravanes en aluminium des années 1940 et 1950 et un yacht « Chris Craft » échoué.
RESTAURATION	« Dot's Diner » sert le petit-déjeuner et le déjeuner entre 7h et 15h, du mercredi au dimanche
HISTOIRE	Un village de caravanes ouvert en 1927, restauré et rééquipé avec des caravanes d'époque en 1995.
LE « PETIT PLUS »	La liberté et le romantisme de la route américaine.

Hot Hot Hot...
Furnace Creek Inn, Death Valley

Furnace Creek Inn, Death Valley

Hot Hot Hot
Sometimes the numbers say it all. 65 meters below sea level. Rainfall less than 5mm a year. Average temperature in June, 48 C. The desert in Death Valley, which straddles the state borders of California and Nevada, is the lowest, driest, hottest place in the United States. Despite its forbidding climate, is is also astonishingly lush and beautiful: strange salt formations rise from its pulverized soil, which changes color from white to grey to shades of brown and purple as the relentless sun makes its way across the sky. When it does rain, purple and gold wildflowers magically sprout from the dust. The Furnace Creek Inn dates back to 1927. It's opening was a bit of a gamble – the property owners, a mining company, were hoping to lure tourists to the area to buffer the fluctuating market demand for their product, borax. While tourists didn't exactly flock to vacation under the white hot sun, they came often enough for the hotel to remain operation for more than 75 years. It's Death Valley National Park's only resort hotel, an oasis of cool adobe, shady palms, and a 70 foot natural spring-fed swimming pool. The desert begins right outside your hotel room door, and you can admire it from a shady white wicker chair over breakfast. If the landscape seems strangely familiar, that's because it is: Death Valley has served the backdrop for dozens of Hollywood and international movies, from Stanley Kubrick's "Spartacus", to Antonioni's "Zabriskie Point".

Book to pack: "The White Heart of Mojave: An Adventure with the Outdoors of the Desert" by Edna Brush Perkins.
The author's amazing tale of her 1920 journey into the Mojave desert seeking to escape civilization and secure voting rights for women.

Furnace Creek Inn	
Highway 190	
Death Valley, CA 92328	
USA	
Tel. +1 760 786 2345	
Fax +1 760 786 2514	
Email: reserve-fc@xanterra.com	
Website: www.furnacecreekresort.com	
www.great-escapes-hotels.com	

DIRECTIONS	Located about 120 miles (195 km) northwest of the Las Vegas, Nevada airport.
RATES	$$$
ROOMS	66 rooms in the original historic Inn, only available in season, from mid-October to mid-May.
FOOD	Breakfast, lunches, and dinners (California-style eclectic menu) served in the Inn Dining Room; afternoon tea in the lobby.
HISTORY	The original Mission-style Inn was designed by LA architect Albert C. Martin, and opened for business in 1927.
X-FACTOR	A cool retreat in the middle of one of the starkest, lowest most desolate landscapes on earth.

Einfach nur heiß

Zahlen sagen manchmal mehr als Worte: 65 Meter unter dem Meeresspiegel. Weniger als 5 mm Regenfall pro Jahr. Durchschnittstemperatur im Juni 48 °C. Die Wüste von »Death Valley« an der Grenze von Kalifornien und Nevada ist nicht nur der tiefstgelegene Punkt, sondern auch der trockenste und heißeste Flecken Erde der Vereinigten Staaten. Das Klima ist zwar extrem, doch ist die Landschaft keineswegs karg und öd. Im Gegenteil: Aus dem sandigen Boden wachsen bizarre Salzformationen, die je nach Sonnenstand weiß, grau, braun und purpur schimmern. Und wenn es ausnahmsweise einmal regnet, wachsen zauberhafte lilafarbene und goldene Wildblumen aus dem Staub.
Das »Furnace Creek Inn« wurde 1927 von einer lokalen Minengesellschaft eröffnet. Die Nachfrage nach dem vom Unternehmen geförderten Borax unterlag großen Schwankungen, und das Geschäft mit den Touristen sollte für eine sichere Einnahmequelle sorgen. Allerdings blieben angesichts der glühenden Hitze die Touristenströme aus. Doch es kamen genug Gäste, um das Überleben des Gasthauses bis heute zu sichern. Das einzige Resort im »Death Valley National Park« offenbart sich als eine Oase mit kühlen Lehmziegel-Häusern, schattenspendenen Palmen und einem 20 Meter langen Pool, der mit Quellwasser gespeist wird. Doch kaum tritt man aus seinem Zimmer, ist man bereits mitten in der Wüste. Wenn man beim Frühstück im Schatten in weißen Korbsesseln sitzt, kann man sie ausgiebig bewundern. Und sollte die Landschaft irgendwie vertraut wirken: Death Valley diente in dutzenden von Hollywood- und anderen Filmproduktionen als Kulisse. Zum Beispiel in Stanley Kubricks »Spartacus« oder Antonionis »Zabriskie Point«.

Buchtipp: »Death Valley Junction« von Albert Ostermaier. Die surreale Geschichte einiger Menschen vor der Kulisse von Death Valley.

Au cœur de la fournaise

Parfois les chiffres parlent d'eux-mêmes. 65 mètres sous le niveau de la mer. Pluviométrie : moins de 5 mm par an. Température moyenne en juin : 48°C. Le désert de « Death Valley », à cheval sur la frontière entre la Californie et le Nevada, est le lieu le plus bas, le plus sec et le plus chaud des États-Unis. En dépit de son climat peu accueillant, il est également incroyablement riche et beau : d'étranges formations salines percent le sol poudreux qui change de couleur, du blanc au gris en passant par des nuances de brun et de mauve, à mesure que le soleil poursuit sa course impitoyable dans le ciel. Quand il pleut enfin, des fleurs sauvages violettes et dorées jaillissent dans la poussière comme par enchantement.
Le « Furnace Creek Inn » date de 1927. Sa création était un pari un peu fou : ses propriétaires, qui exploitaient des mines de borax, espéraient attirer des touristes dans la région afin de compenser la demande fluctuante du marché pour leur produit. Si les vacanciers ne se précipitèrent pas en masse sous le soleil brûlant, il en vint suffisamment pour que l'établissement reste ouvert pendant plus de 75 ans. C'est le seul hôtel de tourisme du « parc national de Death Valley », une oasis offrant la fraîcheur de ses murs en adobe, l'ombre de ses palmiers et une piscine d'eau de source de 20 mètres de long. Le désert commence juste sur le seuil de votre chambre. Vous pouvez l'admirer au frais dans un fauteuil en rotin blanc tout en prenant votre petit-déjeuner. Ne vous étonnez pas si les paysages vous semblent étrangement familiers : ils ont servi de décor à des dizaines de films d'Hollywood et d'ailleurs, de « Spartacus » de Stanley Kubrick à « Zabriskie Point » d'Antonioni.

Livre à emporter : «The White Heart of Mojave: An Adventure with the Outdoors of the Desert» de Edna Brush Perkins. L'incroyable récit de son périple dans le désert Mojave en 1920 pour échapper à la civilisation et assurer aux femmes le droit de vote.

ANFAHRT	Rund 195 km nordwestlich vom Flughafen Las Vegas in Nevada.
PREISE	$$$
ZIMMER	Das historischen Gasthaus verfügt über 66 Zimmer und ist nur in der Saison von Mitte Oktober bis Mitte Mai geöffnet.
KÜCHE	Frühstück, Mittagessen und Abendessen (kalifornische Küche) werden im Speisesaal serviert, der Afternoon Tea in der Lobby.
GESCHICHTE	Das Gasthaus im spanischen Missions-Stil wurde 1927 vom Architekten Albert C. Martin aus Los Angeles entworfen.
X-FAKTOR	Eine coole Oase mitten in einer kargen, verlassenen Wüstenlandschaft.

ACCÈS	Situé à environ 195 km au nord-ouest de l'aéroport de Las Vegas dans le Nevada.
PRIX	$$$
CHAMBRES	66 chambres dans le bâtiment historique d'origine. Ouvert uniquement pendant la saison touristique, de la mi-octobre à la mi-mai.
RESTAURATION	Les petits-déjeuners, déjeuners et dîners sont servis dans la salle à manger ; le thé dans le hall.
HISTOIRE	L'hôtel original, dans le style mission, a été conçu par l'architecte Albert C. Martin et inauguré en 1927.
LE « PETIT PLUS »	Un havre de fraîcheur au cœur de l'un des paysages les plus austères et sauvages de la planète.

In Hot Water, Chilled Out...

Hope Springs Resort, Desert Hot Springs

Hope Springs Resort,
Desert Hot Springs

In Hot Water, Chilled Out

Drive twenty minutes north of Palm Springs, and you reach
the town of Desert Hot Springs, a completely opposite style
of desert oasis. If the signature drink of Palm Springs is the
dry martini, then Desert Hot Springs' preferred libation is
the glass of mineral water, preferably one drawn from one of
the town's dozens of wells that bubble and burble with
health-giving, healing natural spring water. The Agua
Caliente Indians were the first settlers in the area around
Desert Hot Springs, and you can still feel their spirits in the
dry air here, and at the end of streets that suddenly, abruptly,
turn into wild desert brush. It was never a particularly fash-
ionable place – the dozens of little courtyard motels that dot
the area were built mostly in the 1950s and 1960s to serve
the needs of health enthusiasts taking the waters. Almost
unchanged over the years, they now are like vintage can-
vases, waiting to be restored by a new generation of hoteliers
who have come to Desert Hot Springs enchanted by the
water, the high desert, and the nearby Joshua Tree National
Park. Hope Springs is one of those loving renovations – out
front the owner has even kept the original trapezoidal neon
sign that proclaims the property, incorrectly, as "Cactus
Springs". Inside, in a spacious courtyard dotted with cacti
and desert palms, cozy 1940s-style padded lounge chairs
invite you to nap by one of the three thermal bathing pools,
each one heated to a slightly higher temperature. The
rooms, with their simple neutral linens and platform beds,
have a Japanese feel, and most of them open onto a small
patio made private by clever landscaping. No room phones,
no tv. Throw open the French doors, toddle out to the hot
pool, soak, rinse, repeat.

**Book to pack: "Cathedrals of the Flesh: My Search for the
Perfect Bath" by Alexia Brue.**
The adventures of an English woman who recently traveled
the world in search of the ultimate hot spring spa.

Hope Springs Resort	
68075 Club Circle Drive	
Desert Hot Springs, CA 92240	
USA	
Tel: +1 760 329 4003	
Fax: +1 760 329 4223	
Email: manager@hopespringsresort.com	
Website: www.hopespringsresort.com	
www.great-escapes-hotels.com	

DIRECTIONS	8 miles (13 km) north of Palm Springs Airport.
RATES	$
ROOMS	10 rooms; four have kitchens.
FOOD	Continental buffet breakfast only, included in room rate.
HISTORY	Vintage mid-century motel converted to hip haven.
X-FACTOR	Unwind in hot water, in a laid-back vintage mid-century motel.

Chill-out in heißen Quellen

Zwanzig Autominuten nördlich vom kalifornischen Palm Springs liegt eine weitere Wüstenoase, »Desert Hot Springs«. Während Palm Springs das mondäne Leben und den Dry Martini liebt, bevorzugt »Desert Hot Springs« gesundes Mineralwasser, das hier aus dutzenden von Quellen hervorblubbert. Die ersten Bewohner der Gegend waren Indianer des Agua-Caliente-Stammes. Noch immer ist ihr Geist in der trocken-flirrenden Luft zu spüren, besonders dort, wo die Straßen abrupt in der Trockenholz-Wüste enden. »Desert Hot Springs« war nie besonders schick – in den Fünfzigern und Sechzigern reisten vor allem Gesundheitsfanatiker zu den Heilquellen und übernachteten in den kleinen Motels mit den typischen Innenhöfen. Über Jahre hinweg blieben sie praktisch unverändert. Dann zog die Vintage-Welle eine neue Generation von Hoteliers an, die die Motels renovierten und auch von den Heilquellen, der Wüstenlandschaft und dem nahegelegenen Joshua Tree National Park begeistert waren. »Hope Springs« ist eines dieser liebevoll renovierten Motels: Der Besitzer hat sogar das dreieckige Original-Neonschild draußen stehenlassen, obschon darauf der alte Name »Cactus Springs« steht. Im großräumigen Innenhof stehen Wüstenpalmen und kusch-lig-gepolsterte Lounge-Sessel, die zum Faulenzen einladen. Drei Thermalbecken mit unterschiedlichen Temperaturen sorgen für Entspannung. Vertiefen kann man sie nach dem Bad in den Gästezimmern: Mit direktem Zugang auf die Terrasse, einfachen Plattform-Betten und heller Wäsche strahlen sie zen-buddhistische Ruhe aus.

Buchtipp: »Cathedrals of the Flesh: My Search for the Perfect Bath« von Alexia Brue.
Die Erzählungen einer Engländerin auf der Suche nach dem ultimativen heißen Quellbad.

Un bain de jouvence

À vingt minutes de voiture au nord de Palm Springs, « Desert Hot Springs » est une oasis radicalement différente. Ici, la boisson de prédilection n'est pas le martini dry mais l'eau minérale thérapeutique qui gargouille dans les nombreux puits de la ville. Les Indiens d'« Agua Caliente » furent les premiers à s'y installer. Leurs esprits hantent encore l'air sec, errant dans ces rues qui s'interrompent abruptement sur le désert de broussailles. L'endroit ne fut jamais très mondain : la plupart des dizaines de petits motels de la région furent construits dans les années ciquante et soixante pour les fans de médecine naturelle venus prendre les eaux. Restés dans leur jus au fil des ans, ils attendent d'être restaurés par la nouvelle génération d'hôteliers attirés à « Desert Hot Springs » par son eau, le désert et le parc national du Joshua Tree voisin. « Hope Springs » est un exemple de ces relookages inspirés. À l'extérieur, son propriétaire a même conservé l'enseigne d'origine avec l'ancien nom « Cactus Springs ». À l'intérieur, dans une cour spacieuse plantée de cactus et de palmiers, des transats capitonnés style années quarante invitent à la sieste au bord d'une des trois piscines thermales, chacune d'une température différente. Les chambres, avec leur linge neutre et leurs lits juchés sur des plates-formes, baignent dans une atmosphère japonisante. La plupart donnent sur un patio auquel un paysagisme astucieux confère une allure privative. Elles n'ont ni téléphone ni télévision. Ouvrez la baie vitrée, traînez-vous jusqu'à un bassin, trempez-vous, rincez-vous, recommencez.

Livre à emporter : « Cathedrals of the Flesh: My Search for the Perfect Bath » de Alexia Brue.
Les aventures d'une Anglaise qui a récemment sillonné le monde en quête du nec plus ultra en matière de thermes.

ANREISE	Etwa 13 km nördlich vom Flughafen Palm Springs.
PREISE	$
ZIMMER	Zehn Zimmer, davon haben vier eine Küche.
KÜCHE	Frühstücksbüffet, im Zimmerpreis eingeschlossen.
GESCHICHTE	Motel der Moderne, heute schicker Hippie-Hangout.
X-FAKTOR	Entspannung in ultramoderner Umgebung. Eintauchen in warme Heilquellen.

ACCÈS	À 13 km au nord de l'aéroport de Palm Springs.
PRIX	$
CHAMBRES	10 chambres, dont quatre avec cuisine.
RESTAURATION	Buffet continental pour le petit déjeuner uniquement, inclus dans le prix de la chambre.
HISTOIRE	Hôtel des années cinquante converti en refuge branché.
LE « PETIT PLUS »	Décompressez dans l'eau chaude, dans un cadre décontracté et rétro.

Five-star Luxury Kitsch...
Parker Palm Springs, Palm Springs

Parker Palm Springs,
Palm Springs

Five-star Luxury Kitsch

In the 1960s and 1970s, US television was in its prime, and so was TV style – the futuristic, bordering on kitsch home décor of the living rooms of popular TV comedies and talk shows like "The Brady Bunch" and "The Merv Griffin Show". The Parker Palm Springs is the perfect retro-retreat for that generation of American baby boomers who grew up doing their homework in front of the tube, by the light of a Lava Lamp. Step behind the lobby entrance – a striking mid-century "bris soile" wall of latticed concrete, the signature architectural motif of the 1950s Holiday Inn this property once was-and you're suddenly in a luxe, grown-up reinvention of your favorite 70s TV program. The set designer of the show is ceramicist and furniture designer Jonathan Adler, who believes that "minimalism is a bummer", and that "handcrafted tchotchkes are life-enhancing". The public spaces and rooms in the Parker Palm Springs, which is part of the international Le Meridien group, quote diverse sources – there's a touch of the cartoon "The Flintstones" in the floor-to-ceiling freeform concrete room dividers, while the almost-not-quite-tacky blue, green, and olive geometric prints on the chairs of the in-house restaurant "Mister Parker's" work beautifully with mirrored ceilings and chandeliers to create a setting that's Liberace-esque. Adler's playful interiors contrast with the old-fashioned service-intensive ethic of Palm Springs' only 5 star resort – the staff's been ordered, for instance, to immediately offer a picnic lunch to any guest who lazes in one of the resort's hammocks. But will they serve TV dinners?

Book to pack: "Do You Remember TV? The Book That Takes You Back" by Michael Gitter, Sylvie Anapol and Erika Glazer. Kitchy and informative pictorial guide to American classic tv shows from the 1960s and 1970s.

Parker Palm Springs	
4200 East Palm Canyon Drive	
Palm Springs, CA 92264	
USA	
Tel. +1 760 770 5000	
Fax +1 760 324 2188	
Email: reservations@theparkerpalmsprings.com	
Website: www.theparkerpalmsprings.com	
www.great-escapes-hotels.com	

DIRECTIONS	3.5 miles (6 km) south of Palm Springs International Airport.
RATES	$$$
ROOMS	131 Rooms, 12 private one bedroom villas, and the Gene Autry Residence, a home with two bedrooms, living room, dining room, kitchen, two baths and lawn area.
FOOD	Norma's: A five-star diner that serves high-end American "comfort food". Mister Parker's, a 65-seat restaurant with no menus, and a daily changing prix fixe dinner.
HISTORY	Built in the 1950s as a Holiday Inn, it was Merv Griffin's Givenchy Resort and Spa. The Parker Palm Springs was reopened in 2004.
X-FACTOR	Retro chic for grownup American baby-boomers.

Luxus-Kitsch

Das amerikanische Fernsehedekor erlebte in den Sechzigern und Siebzigern einen Höhepunkt. Komödien und
Talk-Shows glänzten mit Studiowohnzimmern, die haar-
scharf am Kitsch vorbei steuerten. Für die Generation der
Baby Boomer, die als Kinder vor der Glotze und neben
einer blubbernden Lava-Lampe ihre Hausaufgaben zu erle-
digen pflegten, ist das »Parker Palm Springs« der perfekte
Retro-Rückzugsort. Eine riesige frei stehende Betonwand
mit durchbrochenem Muster markiert den Eingang. Sie ist
ein Relikt aus den Fünfzigern, als das Hotel der »Holiday-
Inn«-Gruppe angeschlossen war und solche Wände zur
Corporate Identity gehörten. Von hier weg gelangt man in die
Lobby – eine zeitgemäße und luxuriöse Version eines
Siebziger-Jahre-Fernseh-Dekors. Inszeniert hat dieses
Bühnenbild der New Yorker Keramik- und Möbeldesigner
Jonathan Adler im Auftrag der Meridien-Gruppe, der Be-
sitzerin des »Parker Palm Springs«. Von Minimalismus
scheint Adler offensichtlich nicht viel zu halten. Das ganze
Hotel ist ein einziger gigantischer Stilmix: Ein skurriler
Freestyle-Wandtrenner erinnert an den Einrichtungsstil der
»Familie Feuerstein«, und das Restaurant »Mister Parker's«
mit blau, grün, oliv gemusterten, leicht billig wirkenden
Polsterstühlen, verspiegelten Decken und Lüstern würde
selbst Liberace alle Ehre machen. Einzig beim Service kennt
das Haus keinen Spaß. Das einzige 5-Sterne-Resort in Palm
Springs betreibt ihn auf höchstem Niveau.

**Buchtipp: »Do You Remember TV? The Book That Takes You
Back« von Michael Gitter, Sylvie Anapol und Erika Glazer.**
Kitschiges und informatives Bilderbuch über die amerikani-
schen TV-Shows der 1960er und 1970er.

Luxe kitsch cinq étoiles

Dans les années soixante et soixante-dix, la télévision américaine était dans la fleur de l'âge, tout comme son esthétique
illustrée par le look futuriste frôlant le kitsch des séries
populaires et des talk-shows comme le « Brady Bunch » ou le
« Merv Griffin Show ». Le « Parker Palm Springs » est la
retraite rétro idéale pour cette génération de « baby-boo-
mers » qui a grandi en faisant ses devoirs devant le poste, à
la lueur de la lampe à bulles d'huile. Dès que l'on franchit
l'entrée, un surprenant mur en dentelle de béton, motif
architectural typique des « Holiday Inn » des années cinquante dont l'hôtel faisait autrefois partie, on se croirait dans
la version luxe d'un plateau d'émission à succès des années
soixante-dix. Le céramiste et designer Jonathan Adler a signé
le décor, fidèle à sa devise « le minimalisme, ça craint » et
convaincu de « l'effet revigorant des bibelots artisanaux ».
Les espaces communs et les chambres de l'hôtel, aujourd'hui
propriété de la chaîne du Méridien, renvoient à diverses
sources : il y a une touche de la « Famille Pierrafeu » dans
les lignes libres des cloisons en béton des chambres, tandis
que les motifs géométriques bleus, verts et olive – pas tout à
fait ringards mais presque – sur les chaises du restaurant
« Mr. Parker's » s'accordent parfaitement avec le plafond en
miroirs et les lustres pour créer une ambiance à la Liberace.
Les intérieurs pleins d'humour d'Adler contrastent avec l'é-
thique rigoureuse du seul cinq étoiles de Palm Springs :
tous les clients surpris à lézarder dans un des hamacs de
l'hôtel se voient aussitôt proposés un repas pique-nique.
Sert-on aussi des plateaux-télé ?

**Livre à emporter : « Séries télé : De Zorro à Friends, 60 ans de
téléfictions américaines » de Martin Winckler.**
Le romancier américain nous dévoile les coulisses des séries
télé passées, présentes et futures.

ANREISE	6 km südlich vom internationalen Flughafen Palm Springs.
PREISE	$$$
ZIMMER	131 Zimmer, 12 Privatvillen. Gene-Autry-Residenz: zwei Schlaf-räume, Wohnraum, Esszimmer, Küche und Privatgarten.
KÜCHE	»Norma's«, ein 5-Sterne-Restaurant mit einfach-luxuriö-sen amerikanischen Gerichten. »Mister Parker's« mit 65 Plätzen und täglich wechselnden Prix-Fixe-Angeboten.
GESCHICHTE	In den Fünfzigern ein »Holiday Inn«, später das »Merv Griffin Givenchy Resort and Spa«. Im Oktober 2004 als »Parker Palm Springs« wiedereröffnet.
X-FAKTOR	Retro-Schick für Baby Boomer.

ACCÈS	À 6 km au sud de l'aéroport de Palm Springs.
PRIX	$$$
CHAMBRES	131 chambres, 12 villas individuelles avec une chambre à coucher, et la « Gene Autry Residence », une maison individuelle avec jardin.
RESTAURATION	« Norma's », un restaurant cinq étoiles, et « Mister Parker's », un restaurant de 65 couverts avec un menu à prix fixe.
HISTOIRE	Construit dans les années cinquante en tant qu' «Holiday Inn» avant de devenir un hôtel et spa « Merv Griffin's Givenchy ». A rouvert ses portes en octobre 2004.
LE « PETIT PLUS »	Chic rétro pour baby-boomers américains.

Melting into Morocco...
Korakia Pensione, Palm Springs

Korakia Pensione, Palm Springs

Melting into Morocco

Romantic escape is something that many luxury lodgings promise, but few hotels in the world deliver it as effortlessly, and with such perfect detail, as Palm Springs's Korakia Pensione. Here, you pull off the California Interstate highway, pass through the whitewashed gates, and suddenly you are thousands of miles away in Tangiers. Maybe it's because the dry heat and endless sunshine of the Palm Springs desert so closely resemble the white-hot Moroccan sky of Paul Bowles. Or perhaps it is simply because the two original 1924 villas that now form the Pensione were built as marvellous dreams themselves, the fantasies of a Scottish painter named Gordon Coutts. He longed to live in Tangier, but his American wife didn't want to leave the U.S., so he constructed a Tangier of his fantasies in Palm Springs, and baptized it "Dar Marroc". Coutts's artist's retreat attracted a mixed crowd of 1920s bohemians and the hoi palloi – including, it is said, Winston Churchill, who painted in the villa's studio. After Coutts's death the villa languished until it was resurrected by another romantic, owner Douglas Smith, who restored the dilapidated property to its original lush North African/Mediterranean ambience.

The rooms are furnished with pieces collected by the owner from Afghanistan and Thailand. Every one is airy, bright, and whitewashed, and many open to cool, tiled patios. Step through arched portals into courtyards where tiled fountains gently burble, and purple and pink bougainvilla droops overhead: at the Korakia, you may be sleeping in California, but you are dreaming in Morocco.

Book to pack: "The Sheltering Sky" by Paul Bowles.
A journey to the heart of Morocco.

Korakia Pensione

257 S. Patencio Road
Palm Springs, CA 92262
USA
Tel. +1 760 864 6411
Fax +1 760 864 4147
Email: info@korakia.com
Website: www.korakia.com
www.great-escapes-hotels.com

DIRECTIONS	Located in downtown Palm Springs, about 110 miles (180 km) drive east of Los Angeles Airport and 2.7 miles (4.3 km) west of Palm Springs Airport.
RATES	$$
ROOMS	27 rooms and the Orchard House, a one-bedroom house.
FOOD	No dining room; some rooms with kitchens. Breakfast is included and served in the rooms, poolside or in the garden. Moroccan mint tea is served evenings.
HISTORY	1924 Moroccan-style artist's villa restored to its original splendour and opened as a hotel in 1992.
X-FACTOR	Lose yourself in Tangiers without leaving California.

Abstecher nach Marokko

Was viele Luxus-Herbergen versprechen, haben nur ganz wenige: Charme. Eine der schönen Ausnahmen ist die »Korakia Pensione« in Palm Springs. Hier wurde mit wunderbarer Leichtigkeit und Liebe zum Detail eine zauberhafte Welt erschaffen. Bereits die Ankunft ist reizvoll: Man fährt noch ganz normal auf der Haupstraße, durch einen großen, kalkweißen Torbogen, und plötzlich scheint man im marokkanischen Tanger statt in Kalifornien zu sein. Die trockene Hitze und endlos scheinende Sonne über der Wüste von Palm Springs erinnern an die Beschreibung des gleißend weißen Himmels Marokko. Paul Bowles marokkanische Sehnsüchte weckt auch der Geist des schottischen Malers Gordon Coutts, der durch die »Korakia Pensione« weht. Coutts sehnte sich nach Tanger, doch seine amerikanische Gattin wollte unter nicht aus den USA wegziehen. Ein Dilemma, das Coutts 1924 pragmatisch mit dem Bau zweier Villen im marokkanischen Stil löste. Diese Fantasiewelt mitten in der Wüste Südkaliforniens taufte er »Dar Marroc«. Zu seinen Lebzeiten wurde seine Fantasiewelt von den unterschiedlichsten Gästen besucht – Bohemiens, ganz normale Leute, aber auch Persönlichkeiten wie Winston Churchill, der sich im Studio der größeren Villa der Malerei gewidmet haben soll. Nach Coutts' Ableben kümmerte sich lange Zeit niemand mehr um »Dar Marroc«. Der heutige Besitzer Douglas Smith nahm sich dann des verfallenen Anwesens an und verwandelte es zurück in den marokkanischen Traum von damals. Die Zimmer hat er mit Möbeln und Objekten aus Afghanistan und Thailand eingerichtet. Die Wände sind kalkweiß gestrichen, die Räume luftig und hell. Aus einem gekachelten Brunnen, der mit violetten und roten Bougainvillea überwuchert ist, plätschert sanft das Wasser. Willkommen in Marokko!

Buchtipp: »Himmel über der Wüste« von Paul Bowles.
Eine Reise in das Innere Marokkos.

Un rêve marocain

De nombreux hôtels de luxe dans le monde vous promettent un dépaysement romantique mais peu tiennent parole aussi bien que la « Korakia Pensione » à Palm Springs. En sortant de la route principale, on franchit un portail blanchi à la chaux et, soudain, on se retrouve à des milliers de kilomètres de là, à Tanger. C'est peut-être parce que la chaleur sèche et le soleil impitoyable du désert rappellent le ciel chauffé à blanc du Maroc de Paul Bowles. À moins que ce ne soit simplement parce que les deux villas qui forment la « Korakia Pensione » furent construites en 1924 comme deux merveilleux mirages, fantasmes du peintre écossais Gordon Coutts. Il rêvait de vivre à Tanger mais son épouse américaine refusait de quitter les États-Unis. Il s'est donc construit un Tanger issu tout droit de son imagination à Palm Springs et l'a baptisé « Dar Marroc ». Dans les années vingt, ce refuge d'artistes attira une clique bohème et certaines sommités dont, paraît-il, Winston Churchill qui aurait peint dans l'atelier. Après la mort de Coutts, les lieux tombèrent à l'abandon jusqu'à ce qu'un autre romantique, Douglas Smith, ne les ressuscite et ne leur rende leur voluptueuse atmosphère nord-africaine/méditerranéenne.

Dans les chambres, toutes spacieuses, claires et blanches, les meubles ont été rapportés d'Afghanistan et de Thaïlande par les propriétaires. Beaucoup donnent sur de frais patios carrelés. Des arches s'ouvrent sur des cours où glougloutent des fontaines en céramique sous des masses de bougainvillées roses et violettes : à « Korakia », on s'endort en Californie mais on rêve au Maroc.

Livre à emporter : «Un thé au Sahara» de Paul Bowles.
Un voyage au cœur du Maroc.

ANREISE	4.3 km westlich vom Flughafen Palm Springs.
PREISE	$$
ZIMMER	27 Zimmer; das »Orchard House« mit Schlafzimmer.
KÜCHE	Eigenes Restaurant. In den Zimmern kann man kleine Mahlzeiten zubereiten. Frühstück wird in den Zimmern, am Pool oder im Garten unter Zitronenbäumen gereicht. Abends wird marokkanischer Pfefferminz-Tee serviert.
GESCHICHTE	Marokkanische Villa, Baujahr 1924. 1992 stilgerecht renoviert und als Hotel eröffnet.
X-FAKTOR	Eine kalifornische Reise nach Tanger.

ACCÈS	4.3 km à l'ouest du aéroport celui de Palm Springs.
PRIX	$$
CHAMBRES	27 chambres, plus l'Orchard House, une maison individuelle avec une chambre à coucher.
RESTAURATION	Pas de salle à manger; dans les chambres équipées de cuisine on peut préparer des repas simples. Le petit-déjeuner est compris. Du thé à la menthe est servi le soir.
HISTOIRE	Une villa d'artiste de style marocain datant de 1924, restaurée et convertie en hôtel en 1992.
LE « PETIT PLUS »	Perdez-vous dans Tanger sans quitter la Californie.

Roughing It, Softly...
El Capitan Canyon, Santa Barbara

El Capitan Canyon,
Santa Barbara

Roughing It, Softly

The joys of nature are not always joyous for everyone, especially for travellers with an aversion to tiny tents, lumpy sleeping bags, outhouses and the absence of hot and cold running water. El Capitan Canyon is a dream come true for those nature-lovers who wish that nature had better linen and dining facilities. Once a popular private campground located on an ancient Indian ceremonial site just across the road from a magnificent Pacific coast beach, El Capitan was transformed by new owners in 2001 into a "luxury" camp. One hundred sweet cedar cottages with front porches nestle amidst the tall oak and sycamore trees; inside each cottage, a comfy bed, covered in pretty quilts and white cotton sheets, awaits the nature lover. The cottages have full bathrooms, and a few have Jacuzzis. If you'd rather rough it a bit more, there are also 26 airy canvas safari tents with wooden platforms (bathrooms are a short walk down the path). Because El Capitan Canyon is only a ten minute drive from Santa Barbara, if you stay here you can split your time between city and country activities – spend a morning kayaking on the Pacific, and an afternoon shopping in the city's lovely Spanish colonial downtown. Or take a leisurely hike along one of the resort's trails, which lead into the surrounding mountains. The hiking map warns you to watch out for rattlesnakes and lions, a reminder that, even in a luxury campground, Mother Nature has the final word.

Book to Pack: "Cutter and Bone" by Newton Thornburg. Cult-favorite crime thriller set in an evocatively-described Santa Barbara.

El Capitan Canyon

11560 Calle Real
Santa Barbara, CA 93117
USA
Tel. +1 805 685 3887
Fax +1 805 968 6772
Email: terri@elcapitancanyon.com
Website: www.elcapitancanyon.com
www.great-escapes-hotels.com

DIRECTIONS	About 120 miles (195 km) north of Los Angeles, and 17 miles (27 km) northwest of Santa Barbara.
RATES	$
ROOMS	100 cedar cabins and 26 canvas safari tents on wooden decks.
FOOD	Sandwiches, pizzas, bread, wine cheese and other gourmet deli items to eat in or take out at Canyon Market.
HISTORY	Campground opened in 1970; new cabins built in 2000.
X-FACTOR	Camping in hotel comfort.

Rauer Komfort

Ein Aufenthalt in freier Natur ist nicht für alle ein Vergnügen. Vor allem für jene, die enge Zelte ohne fließend warm und kalt Wasser, unförmige Schlafsäcke und Gemeinschaftsbäder fürchterlich finden und beim Campen von richtiger Bettwäsche und Gourmet-Verpflegung träumen. »El Capitan Canyon« lässt den Traum vom guten Leben in der Natur wahr werden. Früher ein ganz normaler, gut besuchter Campingplatz mitten in einer heiligen Indianerstätte und in Strandnähe, wurde daraus 2001 die Luxusversion »El Capitan Canyon«. Hundert Zedernholz-Hütten mit kleinen Terrassen liegen lauschig zwischen Eichen- und Mammutbäumen. In jeder der Hütten steht ein komfortables Bett mit weißer Baumwollwäsche und hübschen Quilt-Überwürfen. Die Holzhütten haben eigene Badezimmer, einige sind sogar mit Jacuzzis ausgestattet. Wer es noch ursprünglicher mag, kann in einem der 26 luftigen Safarizelte auf Holzplattformen übernachten. Die Gemeinschaftsbäder sind nur ein paar Schritte weiter weg. »El Capitan Canyon« liegt zehn Minuten von Santa Barbara, sodass man den Morgen mit Kajakfahrten auf dem Pazifik verbringen kann und den Nachmittag mit einer Shopping-Tour in der historischen spanischen Missionsstadt. Schön auch die Wanderwege, die sich quer durch die Berge des Resorts ziehen. Die Wanderkarte warnt vor Klapperschlangen und Berglöwen: Selbst auf einem Luxus-Campingplatz hat Mutter Natur das Sagen.

Buchtipp: »Geh zur Hölle, Welt« von Newton Thornburg.
Der Kultthriller spielt in Santa Barbara.

Vivre à la dure, en douceur

Les joies de la nature ne font forcément pas le bonheur de tous, surtout quand on a une aversion pour les tentes minuscules, les cailloux sous les sacs de couchage, les latrines à ciel ouvert et l'absence d'eau courante. « El Capitan Canyon » est la réponse rêvée aux amoureux de la nature qui aiment leur confort et bien dîner. Cet ancien terrain de camping privé situé sur un vieux site cérémonial indien, à deux pas d'une magnifique plage du Pacifique, a été transformé par ses propriétaires en 2001 en « campement de luxe ». Cent charmants bungalows en cèdre avec une véranda nichent entre les chênes géants et les sycomores. À l'intérieur vous attendent un lit douillet recouvert d'un édredon et de draps blancs en coton, une vraie salle de bain et, pour certains, même un « jacuzzi ». Ceux qui préfèrent un séjour plus rustique opteront pour une des 26 spacieuses tentes safari en toile perchées sur une plate-forme en bois (avec des bains non loin). Comme Santa Barbara n'est qu'à dix minutes en voiture, vous pouvez alterner les plaisirs de la ville et du grand air, passer la matinée en kayak sur le Pacifique et l'après-midi à faire du lèche-vitrine dans le ravissant quartier colonial hispanique de la ville. Ou encore, faire une randonnée tranquille dans les montagnes environnantes. La carte des sentiers vous met en garde contre les serpents à sonnettes et les pumas, vous rappelant que, même dans un campement de luxe, la nature a toujours le dernier mot.

Livre à emporter : « Fin de fiesta à Santa Barbara » de Newton Thornburg.
Un classique du polar situé à Santa Barbara dont l'atmosphère est particulièrement bien rendue.

ANREISE	Rund 195 km nördlich von Los Angeles und 27 km nordwestllich von Santa Barbara.
PREISE	$
ZIMMER	100 Zedernholzhütten und 26 Safarizelte auf Holzplattformen.
KÜCHE	Sandwiches, Pizzen, Brot, Wein, Käse und andere Delikatessen im »Canyon Market« mit Tischen und Bänken.
GESCHICHTE	Seit 1970 ein Campingplatz, 2000 mit Holzhütten zur Luxusversion ausgebaut.
X-FAKTOR	Campen mit Komfort.

ACCÈS	À environ 195 km au nord de Los Angeles, et 27 km au nord-ouest de Santa Barbara.
PRIX	$
CHAMBRES	100 bungalows en cèdre et 26 tentes safari en toile sur des plates-formes en bois.
RESTAURATION	Le « Canyon Market » propose sandwiches, pizzas, pains, vins, fromages et autres délices à manger sur place ou à emporter.
HISTOIRE	Campement ouvert en 1970 ; de nouveaux bungalows ont été construits en 2000.
LE « PETIT PLUS »	Du camping avec tout le confort d'un hôtel.

Cabin Fever...
Deetjen's Big Sur Inn, Big Sur

Cabin Fever

The first thing you notice, walking up to the main cabin at Deetjen's Big Sur Inn, is the stillness. Tall redwood trees rustle in the breeze, the Pacific Ocean crashes mightily on the rocky cliffs far below. As you check into your room, a Deetjen's clerk hands you an information sheet that advises "Be Considerate. Our walls are paper thin and your neighbor can almost hear you breathe." But the warning seems needless, for here in the middle of redwoods, sea, rocks and spirit, the very atmosphere seems to encourage guests to lower their voices, to listen to one of America's most celebrated natural landscapes. When the two-lane highway was first built along this part of the California coast, on cliffs and bluffs above the ocean, a Norwegian immigrant named Helmuth Deetjen opened a few hand built wooden cabins to shelter travellers making the fabled drive between Los Angeles and San Francisco. As time passed, he built more cabins in his rustic old-world style (the balustrades are hand-carved), and his retreat attracted not only passing sightseers, but the bohemians of San Francisco, the writers and artists and free spirits of the Beat Generation and beyond. Henry Miller hung out here (his old house, now a library, is a few miles up the road), When Deetjen died, his heirs turned the inn into a non-profit organization, in order to keep prices low and preserve the low-key, authentic character of the place. There are no tvs, phones or broadband Internet connections in a Deetjen's cabin room, but there might be a Buddha, and there certainly will be a little diary, where guests can write notes to each other across the decades, like this one: "I never thought I'd sleep in a bed where so many neurotics and bad poets slept before me...otherwise it is very peaceful here. Goodnight"

Book to Pack: "Big Sur and the Oranges of Hieronymous Bosch" by Henry Miller.
The great American novelist's meditation on his life in Big Sur.

Deetjen's Big Sur Inn
48865 Highway 1
Big Sur, CA 93920
USA
Tel. +1 831 667 2377
Fax +1 831 667 0466
Website: www.deetjens.com
www.great-escapes-hotels.com

DIRECTIONS	30 miles (50 km) south of Carmel, California on U.S. Highway 1.
RATES	$
ROOMS	18 rooms, one small house.
FOOD	Breakfasts and continental-style dinners served in the inn's rustic dining room with fireplace.
HISTORY	Built by Norwegian immigrant Helmuth Deetjen on his land in the 1930s.
X-FACTOR	An oasis of stillness and simplicity in one of America's most famous landscapes.

Rustikaler Hüttenzauber

Die Ruhe im »Deetjen's Big Sur Inn« wird einzig vom Rascheln der Bäume und den Wellen, die an die felsigen Klippen des Pazifiks peitschen, gestört. An der Rezeption bekommt der Gast gleich ein Blatt in die Hand gedrückt: »Bitte nehmen Sie Rücksicht auf die anderen Gäste. Unsere Wände sind so dünn wie Papier, ihr Zimmernachbar kann Sie atmen hören.« Der Hinweis entpuppt sich schnell als hinfällig. Die friedliche Atmosphäre lässt automatisch die Stimme senken, und man lauscht andächtig auf die Natur. Als die Straße entlang der Steilküste zwischen Los Angeles und San Francisco gebaut wurde, entwickelte der Norweger Helmuth Deetjen hoch über dem Ozean ein paar rustikale Holzhütten für die Reisenden. Der Ort lockte nicht nur Ausflügler, sondern auch die Künstlerszene der Beat Generation an. Henry Miller pflegte sich hier aufzuhalten (sein ehemaliges Haus, heute eine Bibliothek, steht wenige Kilometer weiter oben). Deetjens Erben gründeten nach seinem Tod eine gemeinnützige Stiftung, um die Zimmerpreise tief zu halten und den authentischen Charakter des Ortes zu bewahren. Fernseher, Telefone oder Internet-Anschlüsse sucht man hier vergebens. Dafür findet man Buddha-Statuen und ein Tagebuch, mit dem die Gäste über die Jahrzehnte hinweg untereinander kommunizieren: »Nicht im Traum hätte ich daran gedacht, einmal eine Nacht in einem Bett zu verbringen, in dem so viele Neurotiker und schlechte Dichter geschlafen haben«, schrieb ein Gast. »Dennoch ist es hier sehr friedlich.«

Buchtipp: »Big Sur und die Orangen des Hieronymus Bosch« von Henry Miller.
Reflektionen Millers über seine Zeit in Big Sur.

L'appel de la nature

Ce qui frappe d'abord, c'est le calme. Le frémissement des hauts séquoias, les puissantes vagues du Pacifique qui s'écrasent au pied des falaises. Avec votre clef, le réceptionniste vous remet une note : « Soyez prévenants. Nos cloisons sont si fines que votre voisin peut presque vous entendre respirer ». C'est inutile car tout ici incite spontanément à baisser la voix et à tendre l'oreille pour écouter l'un des paysages naturels les plus célèbres d'Amérique. Quand la première route a été tracée le long de cette partie de la côte, un Norvégien, Helmut Deetjen, a construit quelques cabanes en bois pour les voyageurs qui effectuaient ce trajet mythique entre Los Angeles et San Francisco. Au fil du temps, il s'est agrandi tout en conservant son style rustique à l'ancienne (avec des balustrades sculptées) et sa retraite a attiré, outre les touristes, la bohème de San Francisco : écrivains, artistes et autres libres penseurs de la génération beat et des suivantes. Henry Miller était un voisin (sa maison, devenue bibliothèque, est à deux pas). À la mort de Deetjen, ses héritiers ont transformé l'hôtel en organisation à but non lucratif afin de conserver des tarifs bas et préserver l'authenticité des lieux. On ne trouve ni télé, ni téléphone ni Internet à haut débit dans les chambres mais, éventuellement, un bouddha et, à coup sûr, un journal où les hôtes peuvent se laisser des messages d'une décennie à l'autre, tel que celui-ci : « Je n'aurais jamais cru dormir un jour dans un lit qui a vu passer tant de névrosés et de mauvais poètes. À part ça... c'est très paisible ici. Bonne nuit. »

Livre à emporter : « Big Sur, sur les Oranges de Jérôme Bosch » d'Henry Miller.
Une méditation du grand romancier américain sur sa vie à Big Sur.

ANREISE	50 km südlich von Carmel, Kalifornien, am US Highway 1.
PREISE	$
ZIMMER	18 Zimmer, ein kleines Haus.
KÜCHE	Frühstück und kontinentales Abendessen im rustikalen Speisesaal mit Kamin.
GESCHICHTE	In den dreißiger Jahren vom norwegischen Einwanderer Helmuth Deetjen erbaut.
X-FAKTOR	Eine Oase der Ruhe und Einfachheit in einer der berühmtesten Landschaften Amerikas.

ACCÈS	À 50 km au sud de Carmel, en Californie, sur l'U.S. Highway 1.
PRIX	$
CHAMBRES	18 chambres, une petite maison.
RESTAURATION	Cuisine continentale ; les petits-déjeuners et dîners sont servis dans la salle à manger rustique de l'auberge, devant la cheminée.
HISTOIRE	Construit par un immigré norvégien, Helmuth Deetjen, sur ses terres dans les années 1930.
LE « PETIT PLUS »	Un havre de calme et de simplicité dans l'un des plus célèbres paysages des États-Unis.

Under a Grass Roof...
Post Ranch Inn, Big Sur

Under a Grass Roof

At the Post Ranch Inn it is easy to disappear from sight. It sits back from the highway, on a mountain ridge overlooking the Pacific Ocean that is invisible to passers-by. Your room is in a cabin or cottage that has been especially designed by local architect Mickey Muennig to blend into and harmonize with the wild natural surroundings on the ranch's 98 acres. There are treehouses on 9 foot stilts (to protect the sensitive roots of the surrounding trees). Cylindrical cottages with mountain views. And for those who like to be, literally, covered by nature, there are five ocean-view cottages with sloped rooftops packed with sod that sprouts grass and wildflowers. Post Ranch Inn was built in the 1990s, after the eco-minded residents of the Big Sur area had passed stringent land-use and zoning rules. It demonstrates that a world class luxury spa resort – and the Post Ranch Inn has won almost every American travel magazine's accolade in this category – can be 100% ecologically sensitive, too. Which is a comforting thought to hold on to as you are lying – no, disappearing into – the massage table at the Post Ranch Inn's spa during your La Stone Massage.

Book to Pack: "Big Sur" by Jack Kerouac.

The Beat Generation author of "On The Road" writes about time spent in a Big Sur cabin.

Post Ranch Inn	
Highway One, P.O. Box 219	
Big Sur, CA 93920	
USA	
Tel. +1 831 667 2200	
Fax +1 831 667 2512	
Email: reservations@postranchinn.com	
Website: www.postranchinn.com	
www.great-escapes-hotels.com	

DIRECTIONS	Off U.S. Highway 1, 150 miles (240 km) south of San Francisco.
RATES	$$$$
ROOMS	30 rooms, in architecturally unique buildings with an ecological bent.
FOOD	Sierra Mar, an award-winning, glass-enclosed restaurant. Breakfast, lunch and dinners of "New California Cuisine" and a 3,000 bottle wine cellar.
HISTORY	Purpose-built eco-resort. Opened in 1992.
X-FACTOR	Maximum luxury and privacy on the Big Sur coast.

Unter einem Dach aus Gras

Einfach mal abtauchen. Dafür eignet sich das »Post Ranch Inn« besonders gut. Das Gasthaus liegt hoch über dem Highway auf einer Bergkante und überblickt den Pazifik, den man beim Vorbeifahren von der Straße gar nicht sehen kann. Die Zimmer sind in einer der Hütten oder einem der Cottages der rund 40 Hektar großen Ranch untergebracht und fügen sich so harmonisch in die unberührte Landschaft ein, wie es ihr Architekt, Mickey Muennig, geplant hatte: Baumhütten stehen auf gut 2,5 Meter hohen Pfählen, um die empfindlichen Wurzeln der Bäume rundherum zu schonen, und zylinderförmige Cottages gewähren freie Sicht auf die Berge. Für Gäste, die Natur pur erleben möchten, gibt es fünf Cottages mit rasenbedeckten Schrägdächern, aus denen Gräser und Wildblumen sprießen. »Post Ranch Inn« wurde in den Neunzigern gebaut, nachdem die ökobewusste Gemeinde Big Sur strikte Raumnutzungsverordnungen verabschiedet hatte. Das Resultat ist ein schönes Beispiel dafür, dass auch ein erstklassiges Luxus-Spa – das »Post Ranch Inn« hat Auszeichnungen der meisten US-Reisezeitschriften erhalten – zu Hundert Prozent ökoverträglich sein kann. Das ist so beruhigend wie eine »La-Stone«-Massage im Spa des »Post Ranch Inn«.

Buchtipp: »Big Sur« von Jack Kerouac.
Der Beat-Generation-Autor von »Unterwegs« schreibt über ein Zeit in einer Hütte in Big Sur.

Sous un toit de verdure

Au « Post Ranch Inn », il est facile de se fondre dans la nature. L'hôtel est situé en retrait de la grande-route, sur une crête rocheuse qui domine le Pacifique tout en restant invisible pour les passants. Les structures ont été spécialement conçues par l'architecte local Mickey Muennig pour disparaître dans le paysage et s'harmoniser avec l'environnement naturel de ce ranch d'une quarantaine d'hectares. Il y a des cabanes perchées sur des pilotis de trois mètres (pour protéger les racines délicates des arbres environnants) ; des cottages circulaires avec vue sur les montagnes ; et pour ceux qui aiment être, littéralement, enfouis dans la végétation, cinq bungalows donnant sur la mer dont les toits inclinés sont plantés de gazons, d'herbes folles et de fleurs sauvages. Le « Post Ranch Inn » a été construit dans les années quatre-vingt-dix après que les habitants à la conscience écologiste de la région de Big Sur eurent adopté des lois strictes en matière d'utilisation des sols et de zonage. Cela prouve qu'un luxueux hôtel et spa de classe internationale (il a été acclamé par pratiquement toutes les revues américaines de voyage) peut être également totalement respectueux de la nature. Ce qui achèvera sans doute d'apaiser vos esprits tandis que vous serez allongé – non, que vous disparaîtrez – sur une table molletonnée pour votre massage à quatre mains.

Livre à emporter : « Big Sur » de Jack Kerouac.
L'auteur emblématique de la génération beatnik décrit ses séjours dans une cabane à Big Sur.

ANREISE	Neben dem US-Highway 1, 240 km südlich von San Francisco.
PREISE	$$$$
ZIMMER	30 Zimmer in einzigartigen Häusern, die nach strikt ökologischen Grundsätzen gebaut wurden.
KÜCHE	Im »Sierra Mar« gibt's Frühstück, Mittag- und Abendessen mit neuer kalifornischen Küche. Das Restaurant mit riesigen Glaswänden hat einen Weinkeller mit 3000 Flaschen und wurde dafür mit einer Auszeichnung bedacht.
GESCHICHTE	Als Öko-Resort gebaut und 1992 eröffnet.
X-FAKTOR	Luxus in der Abgeschiedenheit der Küste von Big Sur.

ACCÈS	Par le U.S. Highway 1, à 240 km au sud de San Francisco.
PRIX	$$$$
CHAMBRES	30 chambres, dans des bâtiments dont l'architecture respecte l'environnement.
RESTAURATION	Le « Sierra Mar », un restaurant primé entouré de parois de verre. « Nouvelle cuisine californienne » servie au petit-déjeuner, déjeuner et dîner. La cave à vins abrite plus de 3 000 bouteilles.
HISTOIRE	Hôtel écologique ouvert en 1992.
LE « PETIT PLUS »	Le summum du luxe et de l'intimité sur la côte de Big Sur.

American Pie...
Madonna Inn, San Luis Obispo

American Pie

To be honest, the Madonna Inn is not everybody's cup of tea. Some travellers, pulling their car off the Interstate highway into the Madonna Inn parking lot, take one look at the giddy building, with its rollicking spiral staircases, multiple balconies, pink, faux-Tudor towers with cupolas and turn the car around and continue driving towards San Francisco. For other travellers, a quick lunch in the Inn's Copper Café, a surreal explosion of bright stained glass, imitation roses, and dozens of Christmas trees that blink and sparkle 365 days of the year, is enough exposure to the Madonna's singular aesthetic. How much kitsch is too much? Fans of the Madonna Inn would say you can never have enough – they relish their nights in one of the Inn's 109 rooms, no two alike. They dream of emerald green carpets, or zebra patterned bedspreads, and read by the light of smiling gold cherub chandeliers. Alex and Phyllis Madonna, the owners, opened their roadside inn on Christmas eve in 1958, and have been decorating and redecorating the place according to their own peculiar vision and taste ever since. The Madonna Inn's location – it is on the highway near San Luis Obispo, exactly halfway between San Francisco and Los Angeles, means that the next customer is always just an exit ramp away. Come to Madonna Inn for the homemade apple pie, or the Danish pastry, baked on the premises; then stay for the cheese.

Book to Pack: "Against Interpretation" by Susan Sontag. Contains "Notes On Camp", Sontag's seminal essay about kitsch.

Madonna Inn
100 Madonna Road
San Luis Obispo, CA 93405
USA
Tel. +1 800 543-9666 or 805 543-3000
Fax +1 805 543-1800
Email: info@madonnainn.com
Website: www.madonnainn.com
www.great-escapes-hotels.com

DIRECTIONS	Located just off U.S. Highway 101, about 2 miles (3 km) south of the U.S. 1 junction, midway between San Francisco and Los Angeles.
RATES	$$
ROOMS	109 rooms, each decorated differently.
FOOD	Classic American steaks and salads at Gold Rush Steak House; American coffeeshop-style dining (breakfast, lunch, dinner, fresh pastries) at the Copper Café.
HISTORY	Family run roadside inn, opened 1958.
X-FACTOR	Kitsch so thick you can almost eat it with a spoon.

Zuckersüßer Kitsch

Das »Madonna Inn« ist nicht jedermanns Sache. Manche fahren vom Interstate 101 kurz auf den Parkplatz des »Madonna Inn«, werfen einen Blick auf das schwindelerregende Gebäude mit spiralförmigen Treppen, unzähligen Balkonen, rosa Disneyland-Türmen und fahren dann schnurstracks weiter Richtung San Francisco. Andere bestaunen bei einem kurzen Mittagessen das exzentrische Dekor des »Copper Café« mit seinen knallbunten Fenstergläsern, künstlichen Rosen und einem Dutzend Weihnachtsbäumen, die das ganze Jahr über blinken und funkeln. Einzig eingefleischte Fans kriegen nie genug vom zuckersüßen Kitsch und genießen die Nächte in einem der 109 völlig unterschiedlich eingerichteten Zimmer in vollen Zügen. Dabei träumen sie von smaragdgrünen Teppichen, Bettdecken mit Zebramuster und lesen ein Buch unter dem Licht goldener Lüster, von denen Cherubine herunterlächeln. Alex und Phyllis Madonna eröffneten ihr Gasthaus an Heiligabend 1958 und richteten es im Laufe der Zeit immer wieder anders, aber immer nach ihrem eigenwilligen Geschmack, ein. Das »Madonna Inn« liegt direkt am Highway 101 in der Nähe von San Luis Obispo, ziemlich genau in der Mitte zwischen San Franciso und Los Angeles. Und wer befürchtet, hier an Reizüberflutung zu leiden, sollte statt einer Übernachtung wenigstens Apfelkuchen oder Dänisch Plunder aus der hauseigenen Bäckerei ausprobieren.

Buchtipp: »Kunst und Antikunst« von Susan Sontag. Ein wegweisendes Essay über Kitsch.

Chantilly à l'américaine.

Pour être sincère, le « Madonna Inn » n'est pas pour tous les goûts. Certains voyageurs s'arrêtent sur le parking de l'hôtel, jettent un regard sur le bâtiment vertigineux avec ses délirants escaliers en colimaçon, ses nombreux balcons, ses tourelles roses en faux Tudor surmontées de coupoles, et font aussitôt marche arrière pour reprendre la route vers San Francisco. D'autres limiteront leur immersion dans l'esthétique singulière du « Madonna Inn » à un bref déjeuner dans son « Copper Café », une explosion surréaliste de vitraux vivement colorés, de roses artificielles et de dizaines de sapins de Noël qui scintillent et clignotent 365 jours par an. Jusqu'où peut-on aller dans le kitsch ? Les fans du « Madonna Inn » vous répondront qu'on ne l'est jamais assez. Ils savourent leurs nuits dans l'une des 109 chambres, toutes différentes. Ils rêvent de moquette vert émeraude, de dessus-de-lit en zèbre et bouquinent à la lumière de lustres dorés ornés de chérubins à l'air ravi. Alex et Phyllis Madonna, les propriétaires, ont ouvert cet hôtel en bordure de route la nuit de Noël 1958 et n'ont cessé depuis de le décorer et de le re-décorer selon leur vision et leurs goûts particuliers. Son emplacement, près de San Luis Obispo, exactement à mi-chemin entre San Francisco et Los Angeles, en fait une halte de choix pour ceux qui prennent la route. Venez à « Madonna Inn » pour goûter sa tarte aux pommes faite maison ou ses pâtisseries viennoises, restez pour le fromage.

Livre à emporter : « Le Kitsch : un catalogue raisonné du mauvais goût » de Gillo Dorflès. Une compilation d'études sur le kitsch sous toutes ses formes, dont une signée du célèbre essayiste autrichien Hermann Broch.

ANREISE	Rund 3 km südlich der Kreuzung US-Highway 101 und US 1 zwischen San Francisco und Los Angeles.
PREISE	$$
ZIMMER	109 Zimmer, jedes verschieden eingerichtet.
KÜCHE	Steaks mit Salat im »Gold Rush Steak House«; amerikanisches Coffeeshop-Menü (Frühstück, Mittag- und Abendessen, hausgemachtes Gebäck) im »Copper Café«.
GESCHICHTE	Seit 1958 Hotel im Familienbesitz.
X-FAKTOR	Kitsch – so klebrig wie Sirup.

ACCÈS	Situé en bordure du Highway 101, à environ 3 km au sud de l'U.S. 1 junction, à mi-chemin entre San Francisco et Los Angeles.
PRIX	$$
CHAMBRES	109 chambres, chacune décorée différemment.
RESTAURATION	Cuisine classique américaine : steaks et salades dans le « Gold Rush Steak » House ; cuisine typique de cafeteria américaine (petit-déjeuner, déjeuner, dîner, pâtisseries faites maison) au « Copper Café ».
HISTOIRE	Hôtel familial en bordure de la route, ouvert en 1958.
LE « PETIT PLUS »	Un kitsch si dense qu'on pourrait presque le manger à la petite cuillère.

Grapes of Style...
The Carneros Inn, Napa

Grapes of Style

Napa Valley has always been a wine-growing center, but lately it has turned into something else: the U.S. capital of the Good Life. Only in the last ten or fifteen years has American culture embraced, wholeheartedly, things epicurean. But thanks to visionary chefs like California's Alice Waters, we are now a nation that knows about soft cheeses, field greens, and the culinary advantages of allowing four-legged creatures to range freely. Napa is the epicentre of the U.S. epicurean revolution, and it is often called the American Tuscany, or Loire Valley, because it is home to the largest concentration of American wineries. Food has followed the wine to Napa, and nowadays the area is renowned as much for its superb restaurants as for its vino. Travelers come here to indulge, to eat, drink and enjoy the fruits of the abundant Napa soil. The Carneros Inn, the newest resort in the area, is something of an anomaly for Napa. While many of the local wineries and lodgings take their stylistic and thematic cues from older European models, this inn, viewed from a distance, looks like a dust-beaten collection of American farmworker's shanties, the sort of place the migrant field hands of John Steinbeck's Grapes of Wrath might have stayed in. But the "agri-chic" aesthetic of this resort development is deceptive; inside the plain, rustic farm cottages with their tin mailboxes and stovepipe chimneys, the Good Life awaits. Open the doors, and the shanty becomes a breezy palace of hardwood floors, vaulted ceilings, wood-burning fireplaces, and showers that open to the stars. From the French windows in your bedroom, the rows of vineyards seem to stretch on forever (which they do: most of Napa's most famous wineries are a stone's throw away from the rocking chair on your front porch.)

Book to Pack: "The Grapes of Wrath" by John Steinbeck. An American classic from one of the literary giants of Northern California.

The Carneros Inn
4048 Sonoma Highway
Napa, CA 94559
USA
Tel. +1 707 299 4900
Fax +1 707 299 4950
Email: info@thecarnerosinn.com
Website: www.thecarnerosinn.com
www.great-escapes-hotels.com

DIRECTIONS	Located about 50 miles (80 km) north of San Francisco on Highway 12-121.
RATES	$$$$
ROOMS	86 guest cottages, each with private patio and garden.
FOOD	The Hilltop Dining Room serves haute California cuisine; the Boon Fly Café serves a more informal breakfast and lunch.
HISTORY	A new resort, opened in 2003: modular tin-roofed guest cottages, built on the site of a former trailer park.
X-FACTOR	Enjoy the "agri-chic" rustic-modernism of Napa valley's newest resort.

Früchte des Genusses

Im Napa Valley wurde, lange bevor es internationale Aner-
kennung fand, Wein angebaut. Doch erst die Entwicklung
zu einer Top-Weinregion machte aus Napa Amerikas wichtigste Lifestyle-Destination. Bis vor zehn, fünfzehn Jahren
waren in den Vereinigten Staaten kulinarische Genüsse wie
Weichkäse, Bio-Gemüse und Fleisch aus Freiland-Tierhal-
tung nahezu unbekannt. Erst weitsichtige Meisterköche wie
Alice Waters vom legendären Restaurant »Chez Panisse« in
Berkeley bei San Francisco weckten die Begeisterung der
Amerikaner für diese Tafelfreuden. Napa ist das Zentrum
der Genussrevolution und wird gerne mit der Toskana oder
dem Loire-Tal verglichen. Nicht zuletzt weil hier landesweit
die höchste Dichte an Weingütern zu finden ist. Sicher aber
auch, weil Napa heute neben Spitzenweinen auch eine aus-
gezeichnete Küche bietet. Viele der Weingüter und Gast-
häuser orientieren sich an europäischen Stilvorbildern.
Ungewöhnlich ist von daher das »Carneros Inn«, das neuste
Resort in Napa. Die Ansammlung traditioneller amerikanischer Landwirtschafts-Baracken erinnert an das Leben der
Landarbeiter, das John Steinbeck in seinem Werk »Früchte
des Zorns« beschreibt. Doch der »Agro-Schick« des Resorts
täuscht. Die einfachen, rustikalen Cottages mit den typisch
amerikanischen Briefkästen aus halbrundem Blech und altmodischen Ofenrohren sind innen luxuriös mit Parkett,
gewölbten Decken, Kaminen und Duschen mit Dachluken
ausgestattet. Und durch die Sprossenfenster kann man den
Blick über die endlosen Weinreben schweifen lassen.

Buchtipp: »Früchte des Zorns« von John Steinbeck

Klassiker der modernen US-amerikanischen Literatur, 1940
mit dem Pulitzer-Preis ausgezeichnet.

Les raisins du bien-être

La vallée de Napa a toujours été une région viticole mais,
récemment, elle est devenue la capitale U. S. de l'art de
vivre. Depuis une dizaine d'années, les Américains s'aban-
donnent sans réserve aux plaisirs épicuriens. Grâce à des
chefs visionnaires tels qu'Alice Waters, ils se sont familiari-
sés avec les fromages à pâte molle, les légumes verts et les
avantages culinaires du bétail élevé en liberté. Épicentre de
cette révolution, Napa est surnommée la Toscane ou la vallée
de la Loire américaine en raison de ses nombreux vignobles.
La gastronomie a suivi et, aujourd'hui, elle est également
renommée pour ses grands restaurants. Les voyageurs viennent ici pour la bonne chère et jouir des fruits de son sol
généreux.
Le « Carneros Inn », récemment inauguré, se distingue des
autres établissements vinicoles et hôtels de la région qui
s'inspirent de modèles européens plus anciens. De loin, il
ressemble à un ensemble de baraques agricoles balayées par
la poussière, du genre qui abritaient les journaliers des
« Raisins de la colère ». Mais son esthétique « agro-chic » est
trompeuse : à l'intérieur des bungalows rustiques, avec leur
boîtes aux lettres en fer blanc et leurs cheminées en tuyau
de poêle, la belle vie vous attend. En ouvrant la porte, vous
découvrez un luxe joyeux, des planchers lustrés, des plafonds voûtés, de grandes cheminées et des douches ouvertes
sur les étoiles. Depuis la baie vitrée de votre chambre, les
vignes s'étendent à perte de vue (la plupart des plus célèbres
vignobles de Napa se trouvent à un jet de pierre du rocking-
chair sur votre véranda).

Livre à emporter : « Les raisins de la colère » de John Steinbeck.

Un classique de la littérature américaine par l'un de ses plus
dignes représentants.

ANREISE	Ungefähr 80 km nördlich von San Francisco auf dem Highway 12-121.
PREISE	$$$$
ZIMMER	86 Gästecottages, jedes mit Privatterrasse und Garten.
KÜCHE	Der »Hilltop Dining Room« serviert erstklassige kalifornische Küche; im »Boon Fly Café« gibt's Frühstück und Mittagessen in zwangloser Umgebung.
GESCHICHTE	Ein neues Resort, 2003 eröffnet, modulare Cottages mit Blechdächern auf einem ehemaligen Campingplatz.
X-FAKTOR	Rustikal-moderner »Landwirtschafts-Schick«.

ACCÈS	Situé à environ 80 km au nord de San Francisco sur le Highway 12-121.
PRIX	$$$$
CHAMBRES	86 bungalows, chacun avec un patio et un jardin privés.
RESTAURATION	Le « Hilltop Dining Room » sert de la haute cuisine californienne ; le « Boon Fly Café » propose des petits-déjeuners et déjeuners plus simples.
HISTOIRE	Nouvel établissement ouvert en 2003 : bungalows modulaires avec toit en fer, construit sur le site d'un ancien village de mobiles homes.
LE « PETIT PLUS »	Goûtez au modernisme rustique « agro-chic » du dernier-né des établissements de la vallée de Napa.

Be Here, Now...
Wilbur Hot Springs, Wilbur Springs

Wilbur Hot Springs, Wilbur Springs

Be Here, Now

Nobody going to San Francisco wears flowers in their hair anymore (except, perhaps, if they are in a wedding party), and the Bay Area is no longer the hippie capital that it was in the 1970s. Nevertheless the social scene in San Francisco remains looser, more tolerant, and more relaxed than in other parts of the U.S. For example, there is the tradition of the Hot Springs Weekend. Newcomers to San Francisco soon discover this local ritual: you drive north for two hours, to Sonoma County, and check in to one of a handful of simple rustic bathing retreats that dot the area. Wilbur Hot Springs is perhaps the most famous of the bunch: a big old Victorian house with simple rooms, a bunkhouse, and a bathhouse where clothing is optional and the sulphurous water in the three pools ranges from hot to hottest (110 degrees Fahrenheit, or 43 Celsius). The retreat dates back to the 1860s, when bathing in hot springs waters for curative purposes became a fad in America. When the fad died out, the retreat languished for nearly a century, but found new life in the 1970s as a center for therapy and detox. Now it's a staple for San Franciscans of a certain age – New Age, that is – who come for the peace and quiet, the 1800 acre nature preserve, the yoga classes and the absence of room keys and electrical outlets. Things to bring (according to Wilbur's manual): a flashlight, a bathrobe, your own food (meals are self-cooked in a communal kitchen), a sense of humor. Oh, and don't forget to pack your karma.

Book to Pack: "Be Here Now" by Ram Dass.
Classic 1970s road-to-bliss manual.

Wilbur Hot Springs	
Wilbur Springs, CA 95987	
USA	
Tel. +1 530 473 2306	
Email: info@wilburhotsprings.com	
Website: www.wilburhotsprings.com	
www.great-escapes-hotels.com	

DIRECTIONS	Located in Colusa County, CA, about 80 miles (130 km) northwest of Sacramento Airport.
RATES	$
ROOMS	One three-bedroom suite, 17 private guest rooms, and one communal bunk room with 11 beds.
FOOD	Bring and cook your own meals in the communal kitchen.
HISTORY	Established on the site of a failed copper mine in 1865 by Ezekial Wilbur; purchased and remodelled in the 1970s by Gestalt therapist Dr. Richard Miller.
X-FACTOR	Drop your clothes and cares in one of Northern California's oldest New Age hot springs retreats.

Im Hier und Jetzt

Heute reist niemand mehr mit Blumen im Haar nach San Francisco – außer vielleicht als Brautjungfer. Die Hippie-Hochburg der siebziger Jahre ist nicht mehr, auch wenn die Leute in San Francisco lockerer drauf sind als in den meisten anderen Städten der Vereinigten Staaten. Ein Überbleibsel aus dieser Zeit sind die Wochenendausflüge zu den heißen Quellbädern der Umgebung. Neu Zugezogene entdecken diese Tradition sehr schnell für sich. Fährt man zwei Stunden mit dem Auto Richtung Norden, kann man in eines der rustikalen Badehäuser von Sonoma County einchecken. »Wilbur Hot Springs« ist wohl das Bekannteste. Die Anlage besteht aus einem alten viktorianischen Holzhaus mit einfachen Zimmern (ohne Elektrizität), einer Baracke und einem Badehaus, in das man auch nackt rein darf. Die drei Becken sind mit schwefelhaltigem, verschieden heißem Wasser bis maximal 43 Grad Celsius gefüllt. »Wilbur Hot Springs« wurde um 1860 gebaut, als heiße Quellenbäder in Amerika »en vogue« waren. Als solche Heilbäder aus der Mode kamen, fristete das Retreat die nächsten hundert Jahre ein trostloses Dasein. In den Siebzigern wurde es dann aus seinem Dornröschenschlaf wachgeküsst und als Therapie- und Entschlackungszentrum wiedereröffnet. New-Age-Fans aus San Francisco pilgern regelmäßig zu den heißen Quellen, um sich im 720 Hektar großen Naturschutzgebiet zu erholen, machen Yoga und genießen, dass es weder Zimmerschlüssel noch Steckdosen gibt. Mitnehmen sollte man gemäß Prospekt: eine Taschenlampe, einen Bademantel, Lebensmittel (die Mahlzeiten bereitet man in der Gemeinschaftsküche selber zu) – und guten Humor!

Buchtipp: »Sei jetzt hier« von Ram Dass.
Klassiker aus den 1970igern. Leitfaden zur Straße der Glückseligkeit.

Ici et maintenant

Plus personne ne met des fleurs dans ses cheveux pour se rendre à San Francisco (sauf, peut-être, pour un mariage) et le Bay Area n'est plus la capitale baba cool des années soixante-dix. Toutefois, l'ambiance y est toujours plus libre, tolérante et décontractée qu'ailleurs aux États-Unis. Prenez par exemple le « Hot Springs Week-End », un rituel local : tout le monde file dans le comté de Sonoma, à deux heures de route vers le nord, dans l'un des établissements thermaux rustiques qui parsèment la région. « Wilbur Hot Springs » est sans doute le plus célèbre : une grande maison victorienne en bois avec des chambres sobres, un dortoir et des thermes où les vêtements sont facultatifs et les trois bassins d'eau sulfureuse vont du chaud au très chaud (43° C). Il date des années 1860, quand les bains thérapeutiques dans les sources chaudes devinrent à la mode. L'engouement passa et la bâtisse sombra dans la torpeur jusqu'à ce qu'elle connaisse une nouvelle vie dans les années soixante-dix comme centre de psychothérapie et de désintoxication. C'est désormais un lieu incontournable pour les San Franciscains New Age, qui viennent pour la paix, le silence, sa réserve naturelle de 720 hectares, ses cours de yoga, et l'absence de clefs et de prises électriques dans les chambres. Le manuel de Wilbur vous conseille de ne pas oublier : une lampe torche, un peignoir, vos repas (que chacun prépare dans la cuisine collective) et votre sens de l'humour. Oh, et n'oubliez pas non plus votre karma.

Livre à emporter : « Ici et maintenant » de Ram Dass.
Guide des chemins de la béatitude des années soixante-dix, devenu un classique.

ANREISE	Rund 130 km nordwestlich vom Flughafen Sacramento.
PREISE	$
ZIMMER	Eine Suite mit drei Schlafzimmern, 17 private Gästezimmer und ein Gemeinschaftszimmer mit 11 Betten.
KÜCHE	Hier wird in der Gemeinschaftsküche selber gekocht. Lebensmittel mitnehmen!
GESCHICHTE	1865 auf einer abgebauten Kupfermine von Ezekial Wilbur gebaut und vom Gestalttherapeuten Dr. Richard Miller in den Siebzigern übernommen und renoviert.
X-FAKTOR	In Kaliforniens ältestem New Age Retreat lassen sich Kleider und Sorgen abstreifen.

ACCÈS	Situé dans le comté de Colusa, en Californie, à environ 130 km au nord-ouest de l'aéroport de Sacramento.
PRIX	$
CHAMBRES	Une suite avec trois chambres ; 17 chambres individuelles et un dortoir de 11 lits.
RESTAURATION	Cuisinez vos propres repas dans la cuisine collective.
HISTOIRE	Construit en 1865 par Ezekial Wilbur ; racheté et reconverti par le thérapeute Richard Miller.
LE « PETIT PLUS »	Dépouillez-vous de vos vêtements et de vos soucis dans l'établissement thermal New Age le plus ancien de la Californie du Nord.

Provence, California...

Auberge du Soleil, Rutherford

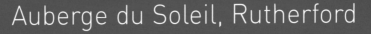

Provence, California

The romantic fantasy of the Napa Valley is that it is America's little piece of the French countryside, a bit of the Rhone valley airlifted to the Pacific coast. In recent years that image has changed, as Napa has acquired its own distinctive Californian identity, but there are still pockets of Napa where you may find yourself lapsing into French while ordering your breakfast. For instance, Auberge du Soleil. At this grand country inn, modelled on a French chateau, it's easy to imagine yourself in Provence; the inn is surrounded by 33 acres of private grounds, filled with vineyards and olive groves, private trails with views of distant mountains. Come in spring, when the wisteria drips from the trellises, or in winter, when the bright yellow mustard flowers bloom in the fields. The Auberge was the first luxury resort to open in the area 30 years ago, and it remains the gold standard for Napa (not surprisingly, it is one of the few American inns in the Relais & Châteaux group). Spacious, tastefully decorated French country-style rooms. World class gourmet restaurant with 1,300 wines (Napa's most extensive wine list). Excellent gym and spa. So delightful that you might not leave the grounds during your stay.

Book to Pack: "A Year in Provence" by Peter Mayle.
Best-selling travelogue about a year spent in French wine country.

Auberge du Soleil
180 Rutherford Hill Road
Rutherford, CA 94573
USA
Tel. +1 707 963 1211
Fax +1 707 963 8764
Email: info@aubergedusoleil.com
Website: www.aubergedusoleil.com
www.great-escapes-hotels.com

DIRECTIONS	65 miles (105 km) north of San Francisco International Airport.
RATES	$$$$
ROOMS	50 one- and two-bedroom suites, two private cottages.
FOOD	In-house restaurant, elegant eclectic California cuisine, tasting menu available.
HISTORY	Opened in 1985.
X-FACTOR	The original, and still the most luxurious of Napa Valley's wine country retreats.

Provence in Kalifornien

Das Napa Valley gab sich lange geschmeichelt, wenn man es mit der französischen Provence verglich, und tat so, als läge ein Stück des Rhônetals direkt an der amerikanischen Pazifikküste. Doch in den letzten Jahren ist Napa reifer geworden und bekennt sich nun ohne Wenn und Aber zu seiner kalifornischen Identität. Noch immer findet man im Napa Valley ein paar Orte mit unverkennbar französischem Flair. Etwa das elegante Landhotel »Auberge du Soleil«, das einem französischen Château nachempfunden wurde. Auf dem 13 Hektar großen Privatgrundstück wachsen Weinreben und Olivenhaine, so als wäre man tatsächlich in der Provence. Die »Auberge du Soleil« liegt, mit tollem Ausblick auf Tal und Berge, mitten an einem lauschigen Hang, und Privatwege laden zu ausgiebigen Spaziergängen ein. Wunderschön auch die Blütenpracht: Im Frühjahr fallen Glyzinien blau über Gitter, und im Winter leuchten gelbe Senfblumen aus den Feldern. Bei seiner Eröffnung vor dreißig Jahren war die »Auberge« noch das einzige Luxusresort im Napa Valley. Trotz Konkurrenz ist es bis heute das stilvollste Haus der Region geblieben (Restaurant und Spa sind übrigens Spitzenklasse) und hat sich – als eines der ganz wenigen Hotels Amerikas – die Aufnahme bei »Relais & Châteaux« redlich verdient.

Buchtipp: »Mein Jahr in der Provence« von Peter Mayle. Liebevoll-bissiger Bericht des britischen Autoren über das erste Jahr in der Provence.

La Provence en Californie

L'image romantique qu'on se fait de la vallée de Napa, c'est celle d'un petit fragment de la vallée du Rhône transplantée par les airs sur la côte Pacifique. Toutefois, ces dernières années, Napa a développé une identité propre typiquement californienne même s'il subsiste quelques poches où l'on peut encore se surprendre à commander son petit-déjeuner en français en se croyant dans un village de Provence. C'est particulièrement vrai à l'« Auberge du soleil ». Cette demeure grandiose, copie d'un château français, est entourée d'un domaine privé de treize hectares plantés de vignes et d'oliviers, sillonné de sentiers d'où l'on peut admirer les montagnes au loin. Venez au printemps, quand les treillis croulent sous la glycine, ou en hiver, quand les fleurs de moutarde jaune vif remplissent les champs. L'auberge fut le premier établissement de luxe à ouvrir dans la région il y a 30 ans et reste l'étalon or de Napa (forcément, c'est l'une des rares auberges américaines du groupe Relais & Châteaux). Des chambres spacieuses décorées avec goût à la française, un restaurant gastronomique de rang international avec un choix de plus de 1 300 vins (la cave la plus complète de Napa), un spa et un centre de remise en forme excellents... c'est un tel ravissement que vous risquez de ne pas sortir du domaine durant tout votre séjour.

Livre à emporter : « Une année en Provence » de Peter Mayle. Le récit humoristique d'un Anglais expatrié dans un terroir bien français.

ANREISE	105 km nördlich vom internationalen Flughafen San Francisco.
PREISE	$$$$
ZIMMER	50 Einzel- und Doppelzimmer, zwei Privat-Cottages.
KÜCHE	Elegante und vielfältige kalifornische Küche; Tasting-Menüs.
GESCHICHTE	1985 eröffnet.
X-FAKTOR	Das erste Luxus-Resort im Weingebiet von Napa Valley ist bis heute der erstklassigste.

ACCÈS	Á 105 km au nord de l'aéroport international de San Francisco.
PRIX	$$$$
CHAMBRES	50 suites à une et deux chambres, deux cottages privés.
RESTAURATION	Le restaurant de l'auberge propose une cuisine éclectique californienne raffinée ; menu de dégustation.
HISTOIRE	Ouvert en 1985.
LE « PETIT PLUS »	La plus ancienne et la plus luxueuse des auberges au milieu des vignobles de la vallée de Napa.

Haute Springs…
Calistoga Ranch, Calistoga

Haute Springs

Napa Valley is best known, of course, for wine, but the name Calistoga is famous on the West Coast because it is a popular brand of mineral water – it is the Vichy, the Perrier of California. In the town of Calistoga, which is located in the northern end of Napa, modest wooden houses and early 20th century public buildings line a main street that appears like something out of an old sepia-toned California postcard. Until recently, Calistoga's main draw was the little inexpensive motels where weekend visitors could take the curative spring waters, and immerse themselves up to the neck in Calistoga's famous, spongy, warm mud baths. But when the Calistoga Ranch, a sister property of nearby Auberge du Soleil, opened in 2004, funky Calistoga became a haute spring. The Ranch, an exclusive retreat of 46 individual lodges located on 157 acres in a valley canyon, has mineral water baths, a spa, and a private-label vineyard. The lodges on the property are spread out, for solitude, and they are large and airy, with floor to ceiling windows that provide endless views of surrounding vineyards, and blur the boundaries between in- and outdoors. So in-tune are the lodges to the natural setting, that many were constructed around the twisted, ancient oak trees that dot the property. Sit back in your lodge, admire the ancient oak that emerges from beneath your deck, and enjoy a glass of your favorite Calistoga beverage: wine, or water.

Book to Pack: "The Accidental Connoisseur: An Irreverent Journey Through the Wine World" by Lawrence Osborne. 2004 American bestseller that chronicles the author's journey through wineries in France, Italy and California.

Calistoga Ranch
580 Lommel Road
Calistoga, CA 94515
USA
Tel. +1 707-254-2800
Fax +1 707-254-2888
Email : reservations@calistogaranch.com
Website: www.calistogaranch.com
www.great-escapes-hotels.com

DIRECTIONS	70 miles (115 km) north of San Francisco International Airport.
RATES	$$$$
ROOMS	46 guest lodges.
FOOD	Dining in the Lakehouse, featuring fine California cuisine and private-label wines, or privately in one's own lodge.
HISTORY	Newly built, opened in 2004.
X-FACTOR	Maximum opulence in California wine country.

Premium-Quelle

Das Napa Valley kennt man vor allem wegen seiner Weine. Doch es gibt dort auch andere Schätze. Zum Beispiel Mineralwasser aus den Quellen von Calistoga am nördlichen Ende des Napa Valley. An der US-Westküste ist es so bekannt wie Perrier oder Vichy in Frankreich. Bescheidene Holzhäuser und Gebäude aus dem frühen 20. Jahrhundert säumen die Hauptstraße des Ortes – eine Szenerie wie auf einer alten, vergilbten Postkarte. Noch bis vor kurzem waren in Calistoga preisgünstige Motels und Wochenendgäste, die Heilwasser tranken und ihre Körper in warme Schlammbäder steckten, die einzige Attraktion. Mit der Eröffnung der »Calistoga Ranch« 2004, die zum nahegelegenen Luxusresort »Auberge du Soleil« gehört, ist das bis dahin unglamouröse Calistoga zur Erstklasse-Destination geworden. Die Ranch, ein exklusives Retreat in einer Schlucht auf 63 Hektar, besteht aus 46 individuellen Lodges, Mineralwasserbädern, einem Spa und einem privaten Weinberg. Die Lodges sind über das ganze Grundstück verteilt, sodass man ungestört bleibt. Sie sind alle groß, luftig mit raumhohen Fenstern, durch die man freie Sicht auf die Rebberge genießt. Manche sind sogar um knorrige, alte Eichen herum gebaut. Hier verwischt Innen- und Außenraum zu einem harmonischen Ganzen.

Buchtipp: »Die Architektur des Weines. Baukunst und Weinbau im Bordeaux und im Napa-Valley« von Dirk Meyhöfer.

Illustrierte Geschichte über amerikanische Weinbauern wie Robert Mondavi und ihre Zusammenarbeit mit Winzern aus dem Bordeaux.

Baigner dans le luxe

La vallée de Napa est surtout renommée pour ses vins mais Calistoga est connue sur toute la côte Ouest comme une eau minérale, équivalent californien de la Vichy ou du Perrier. Dans la ville du même nom, tout au nord de la vallée, de modestes maisons en bois et des bâtiments publics du début du 20ᵉ siècle bordent une rue principale qui semble sortie d'une vieille carte postale sépia. Jusqu'à récemment, son attrait principal était ses hôtels bon marché accueillant les visiteurs venus prendre les eaux le temps d'un week-end et barboter dans ses célèbres bains de boue chauds. Mais depuis que le « Caligosta Ranch », pendant de « l'Auberge du Soleil » voisine, a ouvert ses portes en 2004, Caligosta la malodorante a découvert le grand luxe. Cette élégante retraite de 46 bungalows individuels éparpillés sur 63 hectares au creux d'un canyon possède des thermes minérales, un centre de beauté et son propre vignoble. Spacieux, les bungalows sont éloignés les uns des autres pour préserver l'intimité, avec des baies vitrées qui offrent des vues à l'infini sur les vignes, brouillant les limites entre l'intérieur et l'extérieur. Ils sont tellement en harmonie avec leur environnement que certains sont construits autour des vieux chênes qui parsèment le domaine. Asseyez-vous confortablement, contemplez les troncs anciens qui émergent sous votre terrasse et savourez votre boisson de Calistoga préférée, vin ou eau.

Livre à emporter : « Guide Paumard des grands vins du Monde 2005-2006 » de Bruno Paumard.

Guide pratique et sans complaisance signé d'un expert œnologue.

ANREISE	115 km nördlich vom internationalen Flughafen San Francisco.
PREISE	$$$$
ZIMMER	46 Gästelodges.
KÜCHE	Erstklassige kalifornische Küche und Weine vom hauseigenen Weinberg im »Lakehouse«. Mahlzeiten werden auf Wunsch auch in den Gästelodges serviert.
GESCHICHTE	Neues Resort, 2004 eröffnet.
X-FAKTOR	Üppiges Leben im kalifornischen Weingebiet.

ACCÈS	À 115 km au nord de l'aéroport international de San Francisco.
PRIX	$$$$
CHAMBRES	46 bungalows individuels.
RESTAURATION	On peut dîner dans le « Lakehouse », qui propose un menu gastronomique californien arrosé de crus locaux, ou se faire servir dans ses appartements.
HISTOIRE	Récemment construit, inauguré en 2004.
LE « PETIT PLUS »	L'opulence maximum dans le pays des vins californiens.

Jaw-Dropping...
The Ahwahnee, Yosemite National Park

The Ahwahnee, Yosemite National Park

Jaw-Dropping

The Yosemite Valley, a place of bare, dramatic, granite mountains and cliffs, of high waterfalls and giant Sequoia trees, has been stunning visitors with its grandeur for thousands of years. (The Miwok Indians called this place, "Ahwahnee", or "Place of the Gaping Mouth"). So compelling is the area's beauty that in 1864, during the worst battles of the American Civil War, President Abraham Lincoln took time out to sign the decree which set Yosemite aside as America's first nature preserve. The Ahwahnee lodge was constructed in 1927, within the boundaries of the park, to encourage well-heeled visitors to come to this remote and often desolate area. It is a grand hotel, in the opulent turn of the century style, with massive open public spaces (the hotel's Great Lounge is a 77 feet long, 51 feet wide cathedral of a room with 24-foot-high ceilings, ten floor-to-ceiling windows and a profusion of wrought-iron chandeliers). Perhaps the Ahwahnee's architects were so awed by the famous Yosemite landmarks visible from the hotel's location – the Half Dome, the Yosemite Falls, and Glacier Point – that they designed their interiors to match the scale of the great outdoors. In any case, this grand hotel (with grounds designed by Frederick Law Olmstead) has survived economic booms and busts, the wear and tear of decades, and the ever-present threat of fire in the forest (the Ahwahnee's "redwood" façade is actually poured concrete that has been painted to look like wood!) As the Ahwahnee nears its eightieth year, it has become as much of an icon as Yosemite's natural wonders.

Book to Pack: "The Yosemite" by John Muir.
Essays by the distinguished American naturalist responsible for the creation of Yosemite Park.

The Ahwahnee	
P.O. Box 578	
Yosemite National Park	
California 953 89	
USA	
Tel. +1 801 559 4884	
Email: yoseres@DNCinc.com	
Website: www.yosemitepark.com	
www.great-escapes-hotels.com	

DIRECTIONS	One mile (1.5 km) east of Yosemite Village, in Yosemite National Park.
RATES	$$$
ROOMS	99 rooms and 24 cottages.
FOOD	Huge resort dining room serving traditional American food at breakfast, lunch and dinner.
HISTORY	Originally built in 1927 as a "modern luxury hotel" inside the Yosemite National Park. Landscaping by Frederick Law Olmstead. Remodeled in 2004.
X-FACTOR	A grand old American classic, surrounded by some of the continent's most heartstopping scenery.

Atemberaubend

Das Yosemite Valley mit seinen spektakulären Granitfelsen, in die Tiefe stürzenden Wasserfällen und riesigen Mammutbäumen lässt die Herzen der Besucher seit Jahrtausenden höher schlagen. Indianer des Miwok-Stammes nennen den Ort »Ahwahnee« oder »Offen stehender Mund«. Die Schönheit des Tales ist atemberaubend. Sogar Präsident Abraham Lincoln ließ sich von ihr einnehmen. Obschon mit dem amerikanischen Bürgerkrieg beschäftigt, unterzeichnete er ein Dekret, das aus Yosemite das erste Naturschutzgebiet der Vereinigten Staaten machen sollte. Die »Ahwahnee«-Lodge wurde 1927 mitten im Nationalpark gebaut, um gutbetuchte Besucher in die einsame Gegend zu locken. Als großzügiges Grand Hotel konzipiert, spiegelt das Haus den opulenten Stil der letzten Jahrhundertwende wider. Die Hotelhalle erinnert an eine Kathedrale – 24 Meter lang, 16 Meter breit, 7,5 Meter hohe Decken, zehn raumhohe Fenster und überall schmiedeeiserne Lüster. Es scheint, als ob die Architekten von »Ahwahnee« den großartigen Sehenswürdigkeiten rund ums Haus, dem »Half Dome«, den »Yosemite Falls« und dem »Glacier Point«, mit ebenso grandiosen Räumlichkeiten begegnen wollten. Das Grand Hotel hat gute und schlechte Zeiten erlebt, Wind, Wetter und der ständigen Brandgefahr getrotzt. Die Fassade des Hauses ist deshalb auch nicht aus echtem Holz, sondern im Rot der Bäume angemalter Beton. Bald feiert die »Ahwahnee« Lodge ihren Achtzigsten und gehört mittlerweile zu den Sehenswürdigkeiten von Yosemite – genau wie die Naturwunder.

Buchtipp: »The Yosemite« von John Muir.
Essays vom angesehenen Umweltschützer, der sich für den Schutz des Yosemite-Parks einsetzte.

Buchtipp: »Der John Muir Trail« von Johann Schinabeck.
Beschreibt den beliebten 350 km langen Wanderweg, der nach dem Umweltschützer John Muir benannt wurde, zwischen dem Yosemite-Tal und dem Mount Whitney in Kalifornien.

Bouche bée

La vallée du Yosemite, avec ses spectaculaires massifs granitiques nus, ses falaises, ses cascades, ses séquoias géants, sidère ses visiteurs par sa splendeur depuis des millénaires. Les Indiens Miwok l'avaient baptisée « Ahwahnee », « lieu de la bouche bée ». Sa beauté est si envoûtante qu'en 1864, au cours des heures les plus sanglantes de la guerre de Sécession, Abraham Lincoln prit le temps de signer un décret faisant d'elle la première réserve naturelle du pays. Le « Ahwahnee » a été construit en 1927, en lisière du parc, afin d'attirer les touristes fortunés dans ce coin reculé et sauvage. C'est un grand hôtel dans le style opulent du début du siècle, avec des salles de réception ouvertes et spacieuses (le grand salon fait 24 mètres de long, 16 mètres de large, 7,5 mètres de haut, avec dix fenêtres allant du sol au plafond et une profusion de lustres en fer forgé). Ses architectes durent être si impressionnés par les monuments naturels célèbres visibles depuis le site – le « Half Dome », les « Yosemite Falls », le « Glacier Point » – qu'ils conçurent les intérieurs aux proportions du paysage. Les jardins furent dessinés par Frederick Law Olmstead. L'établissement a survécu aux aléas de l'économie, aux outrages du temps et à la menace omniprésente des incendies de forêt (la façade en « séquoia » est en fait en béton peint en trompe-l'œil de bois !).
Aujourd'hui, à l'aube de ses 80 ans, il est devenu un monument à part entière, au même titre que les merveilles naturelles qui l'entourent.

Livre à emporter : « Un été dans la Sierra » de John Muir.
Le célèbre naturaliste américain à l'origine de la création du parc raconte son voyage pour accompagner des moutons en transhumance.

ANREISE	1,5 km östlich von Yosemite Village im Yosemite-Nationalpark.
PREISE	$$$
ZIMMER	99 Zimmer und 24 Cottages.
KÜCHE	Im riesigen Speisesaal der Lodge wird traditionell amerikanisches Frühstück, Mittag- und Abendessen serviert.
GESCHICHTE	1927 als modernes Luxushotel im Yosemite-Nationalpark gebaut. Landschaftsarchitekt: Frederick Law Olmstead. 2004 Renovierung.
X-FAKTOR	Amerikanischer Klassiker mitten in einer der spektakulärsten Landschaften des Kontinents.

ACCÈS	À 1,5 km à l'est de Yosemite Village, dans le parc national du Yosemite.
PRIX	$$$
CHAMBRES	99 chambres et 24 bungalows.
RESTAURATION	Immense salle à manger où l'on sert une cuisine traditionnelle. Petits-déjeuners, déjeuners et dîners.
HISTOIRE	Construit en 1927 comme «hôtel moderne de luxe» dans le parc national du Yosemite. Jardins dessinés par Frederick Law Olmstead. Réaménagé en 2004.
LE « PETIT PLUS »	Un grand classique américain, au cœur de l'un des paysages les plus époustouflants du continent.

"Vild Vest" ...
Dunton Hot Springs, Dolores

"Vild Vest"

Who buys an entire ghost town? Christoph Henkel, the heir
to the German soap and chemical company fortune, came
upon the ruins of what is now Dunton Hot Springs in the
early 1990s, during a ski trip to nearby Telluride, Colorado.
The ramshackle cabins and former saloon along the Dolores
River in a breathtaking mountain valley had been a thriving
gold miner's camp in the 1890s. Still, you had to have a lot
of imagination to see the grand old rough and tumble days
of Dunton in the ruins that remained. But Henkel did: he
had grown up reading the fantasy Western tales of the German writer Karl May (which were indeed fantasies, since
May never visited the U.S. in his life). As he walked through
the ghost town, Henkel had a flash of inspiration. He
bought the entire town for just over 1 million dollars, and
began recreating his own version of May's "vild vest." As you
first enter the lonely valley, the sight of Dunton's painstakingly weatherbeaten log cabins filled with museum-quality
art and the luxury teepees outfitted with hot tubs may seem
a bit too perfect, too cinematic (Henkel, also a film producer,
has created a very high-end movie set). But any misgivings
one might have about the Ralph Lauren-ness of it all quickly
vanish, lulled away by the silence of the stunning valley, the
million stars overhead, and by the heat of Dunton's abundant natural hot springs, which burble up in steamy pools
amidst snow-dusted fields. At Dunton, foreign inspiration
has revived an American classic.

Book to Pack: "Winnetou the Apache Knight" by Karl May.
Fantasy novel of the American West by the famous German
author.

Dunton Hot Springs
P.O. Box 818
52068 County Road
Dolores, CO 81323
USA
Tel. +1 970 882 4800
Fax +1 970 882 7474
Email: info@duntonhotsprings.com
Website: www.duntonhotsprings.com
www.great-escapes-hotels.com

DIRECTIONS	About 30 miles (50 km) southeast of Telluride, Colorado airport.
RATES	$$$
ROOMS	12 log cabins and three teepees.
FOOD	Local organic foods prepared by in-house gourmet chef, served in Dunton's original saloon.
HISTORY	Former mining camp town restored and transformed into exclusive resort.
X-FACTOR	Where else in the world can you sleep in a teepee that has a hot tub?

»Wild-West«-Fantasien

Auf die Idee, eine Geisterstadt zu kaufen, kommt man nicht
einfach so. Doch Christoph Henkel, Erbe des gleichnamigen
deutschen Seifen- und Chemikalienunternehmens, hatte in
den Neunzigern beim Anblick der Ruinen von »Dunton Hot
Springs« eine zündende Idee. Er entdeckte das ehemalige
Goldminen-Camp, das um 1890 seine Blütezeit erlebte, während eines Skiurlaubs im nahen Telluride, Colorado. In seiner Fantasie machte er aus den zerfallenen Häusern (mit
Saloon!) am Dolores River wieder den glorreichen Ort aus
den Zeiten des Goldrauschs. Henkels Vorstellungskraft
kommt nicht von ungefähr. Er wuchs mit den »Wild-West«-
Geschichten von Karl May auf, der kein einziges Mal in den
USA war und all seine Indianer- und Cowboygeschichten
erfand. Christoph Henkel kaufte kurzerhand die alte
Geisterstadt für etwas mehr als 1 Million Dollar und machte
sich daran, seine Version von Karl Mays Wildem Westen
umzusetzen. Heute stehen die Holzhütten in diesem einsa-
men, wunderschönen Tal immer noch verwittert da – aber
luxuriös ausgestattet und voller museumsreifer Kunst. Die
Szenerie zusammen mit den Luxus-Tipis mit eigenen Bade-
wannen sieht aus wie ein Ralph-Lauren-Stillleben und mag
fast zu perfekt, zu cineastisch wirken. Henkel, der auch als
Filmproduzent tätig ist, hat hier aber nur auf den ersten
Blick eine einzige, große Filmkulisse erschaffen. Die Stille
im atemberaubend schönen Tal, die leuchtenden Sterne am
dunklen Himmel und die dampfenden heißen Quellen, die
sich im Schnee zu Becken sammeln, können nicht mal im
Film so zauberhaft sein.

Buchtipp: »Winnetou« von Karl May.
»Wild-West«-Fantasien des berühmten deutschen Autors.

« L'ouest sôfache »

Qui irait s'offrir toute une ville fantôme ? Christoph Henkel,
héritier d'un empire allemand de savons et de produits chi-
miques, est tombé sur les ruines de « Dunton Hot Springs »
au début des années quatre-vingt-dix, alors qu'il skiait non
loin à Telluride dans le Colorado. Vers 1890, ces cabanes
branlantes et l'ancien saloon bordant le Dolores abritaient
une colonie prospère de chercheurs d'or. Il fallait quand
même pas mal d'imagination pour visualiser la grande époque du « Far West » dans les vestiges délabrés. Mais Henkel
avait grandi en lisant les westerns fabuleux du romancier allemand Karl May (qui n'a jamais mis les pieds en Amérique !).
En se promenant dans la ville désertée, il eut une vision. Il
la racheta pour un million de dollars et s'attela à recréer
« l'ouest sôfache » de May. En pénétrant dans la vallée isolée,
on peut trouver que les cabanes minutieusement patinées
par le temps remplies d'art de qualité et les tipis de luxe
équipés de jacuzzis sont un peu trop parfaits et théâtraux
(également producteur de cinéma, Henkel a créé un plateau
de cinéma haut de gamme). Mais le chic genre Ralph Lauren
s'efface rapidement devant le silence, la splendeur du paysage, les millions d'étoiles dans le ciel et la chaleur des abon-
dantes sources chaudes qui gargouillent dans des bassins
fumants au milieu des prés saupoudrés de neige. À Dunton,
une inspiration venue d'ailleurs fait revivre un classique
américain.

**Livre à emporter: « Winnetou, l'homme de la prairie » de Karl
May.**
Roman sur l'Ouest américain par le célèbre auteur allemand.

ANREISE	Zirka 50 km südöstlich vom Flughafen Telluride in Colorado.
PREISE	$$$
ZIMMER	12 Log-Cabins und drei Tipis.
KÜCHE	Bio-Gourmet-Küche im ehemaligen »Saloon«.
GESCHICHTE	Ehemaliges Minen-Camp, in den Neunzigern zu einem exklusiven Resort renoviert und umgebaut.
X-FAKTOR	Wo sonst auf der Welt gibt es Tipis mit Badewannen?

ACCÈS	À environ 50 km au sud-est de l'aéroport de Telluride, dans le Colorado.
PRIX	$$$
CHAMBRES	12 cabanes en rondins de bois et trois tipis.
RESTAURATION	Plats bios avec des ingrédients locaux préparés par le grand chef maison, servis dans le « saloon ».
HISTOIRE	Ancienne colonie de chercheurs d'or restaurée et conver-tie en complexe hôtelier de luxe.
LE « PETIT PLUS »	Existe-t-il un autre endroit au monde où vous pouvez dormir dans un tipi équipé d'un jacuzzi ?

Ski and Be Seen...
Sky Hotel, Aspen

Ski and Be Seen

You come to Aspen to ski in the fast lane; the Colorado resort town, nestled in the Rockies, has long been an enclave
for the glitterati, a place that boasts a disproportionate number of people who appear in the pages of People (magazine).
In Aspen, the snow is cold, but the nightlife is cool. So your
base camp location is important, and the Sky Hotel is one of
the most stylish bases in Aspen. It's not a luxury resort – the
owners, the Kimpton Group, specialize in affordable hip
hotels – but it has attitude: Leopard print robes and rooms
with bright yellow walls and faux-fur throws. The in-room
entertainment centers have Nintendo games, and if you can't
bear to go on a ski trip without your dog, no problems here:
the Sky Hotel has a special canine package that includes an
in-room doggy bed and breakfast. The Sky Hotel's center is
its restaurant-cum-lounge, 39 Degrees, where techno and
electronica music thrum in the background, and guests
order round after round of the house signature cocktail, the
"Botox Martini". This oh-so-chilled-out hotel also offers a
heated pool, and – in case the hip atmosphere leaves you
feeling a bit breathless – in-room canisters of oxygen.

**Book to Pack: "Fear and Loathing in Las Vegas: A Savage
Journey to the Heart of the American Dream" by Hunter S.
Thompson.**
The most important work by the late American essayist and
Aspen's most famous resident.

Sky Hotel	DIRECTIONS	4 miles (6.5 km) southeast of Aspen Airport.
709 East Durant Avenue	RATES	$$$
Aspen, CO 81611	ROOMS	90 guest rooms.
USA	FOOD	39 Degrees restaurant and bar serves eclectic American food from breakfast until late-night. Cocktails and electronica music in the Lounge.
Tel. +1 970 925 6760		
Fax +1 970 925 6778		
Email: guestloyalty@kimptongroup.com	HISTORY	Old ski lodge converted to boutique hotel in 2002 by the Kimpton group, a San Francisco based chain of design hotels.
Website: www.theskyhotel.com		
www.great-escapes-hotels.com	X-FACTOR	South Beach with skis.

South Beach Style

In Aspen, Colorado, liebt man rasante Pisten-Fahrten – sie passen gut zum Lifestyle der Erfolgreichen. Der Ferienort in den Rocky Mountains, beliebt bei den Schönen und Reichen, brüstet sich gerne mit den Prominenten aus den Klatschspalten, die hier ihren Winterurlaub genießen. Während sie sich tagsüber auf den Pisten den kühlen Wind um die Nase wehen lassen, bringt sie das Nachtleben hier zum Brodeln. Entscheidend ist in Aspen, den richtigen Ort als Absteige zu wählen. Im »Sky Hotel« ist man sicher an einer richtigen Adresse. Es gehört zu den gestyltesten Unterkünften im Ort und, obschon kein Haus der Luxuskategorie, hat es durchaus Allüre. Die Wände der Zimmer sind leuchtend gelb, die Bettdecken aus Imitationspelz, und die Bademäntel beeindrucken mit Leopardenprints. Eine ausgeklügelte Unterhaltungselektronik ist sogar mit Nintendo-Spielen bestückt. Auch Hundenarren kommen hier auf ihre Kosten. Wem es das Herz bricht, seinen Hund zurückzulassen, darf hier auf Verständnis zählen. Das »Sky Hotel« bietet Hunde-Packages mit extra Bettchen im Zimmer und einem Spezialfrühstück für Fido an. Herzstück des Hotels ist die Restaurant-Lounge »39 Degrees«. Hier schlürfen die Gäste zu Technobeats und Elektronika an einem »Botox Martini«. Ein geheizter Pool sorgt für Entspannung, und jedes Zimmer ist mit einem Sauerstoffkanister ausgerüstet. Wohl für Gäste, bei denen der Hipness-Faktor zu leichten Atemstörungen führt.

Buchtipp: »Angst und Schrecken in Las Vegas« von Hunter S. Thompson.
Das wichtigste Werk des Erfinders des Gonzo-Journalismus, der in Aspen lebte.

Skier et être vu

On va à Aspen pour skier beau. La station de sports d'hiver du Colorado, nichée au cœur des Rocheuses, depuis longtemps repaire des riches et célèbres, compte la plus forte concentration de personnalités faisant les beaux jours de la presse people. À Aspen, où la neige est froide mais les nuits torrides, il est important de bien choisir son quartier général. Le « Sky Hotel » est le plus chic de tous. Appartenant à la chaîne Kimpton, spécialisée dans les hôtels abordables mais branchés, ce n'est pas un établissement de luxe mais il a une allure folle : chambres et peignoirs assortis en léopard, murs jaune vif et jetés de lit en fausse fourrure. Les postes de télévision dans les chambres sont pourvus de consoles Nintendo et, si vous ne supportez pas de skier sans votre chien, des lits spéciaux et des petits-déjeuners ont été prévus rien que pour lui. Le cœur du Sky est sa salle de restaurant / salon, le « 39 Degrees », où la techno et la musique électronique ronronnent en fond sonore et où l'on peut siroter à loisir le cocktail maison, le « Botox Martini ». Cet hôtel ô combien cool possède également une piscine chauffée et, si autant de branchitude vous laisse le souffle court, les chambres sont équipées de masques à oxygène.

Livre à emporter : « Las Vegas parano » d'Hunter S. Thompson.
L'œuvre la plus importante du célèbre essayiste américain et résident d'Aspen, aujourd'hui disparu.

ANREISE	6,5 km südöstlich vom Flughafen Aspen.
PREISE	$$$
ZIMMER	90 Gästezimmer.
KÜCHE	Restaurant-Bar »39 Degrees« mit amerikanischer Küche vom Frühstück bis zum Mitternachtsmahl. Cocktails und Elektronica in der Lounge.
GESCHICHTE	Alte Skihütte, 2002 von der Kimpton-Gruppe aus San Francisco zu einem Boutique-Hotel umgebaut.
X-FAKTOR	South Beach in den Bergen.

ACCÈS	À 6,5 km au sud-est de l'aéroport d'Aspen.
PRIX	$$$
CHAMBRES	90 chambres.
RESTAURATION	Le restaurant et bar « 39 Degrees » propose une carte éclectique de cuisine américaine et sert le petit-déjeuner jusqu'à tard dans la nuit. Cocktails et musique électronique dans le salon.
HISTOIRE	Ancien gîte de skieurs reconverti en 2002 par le groupe Kimpton, une chaîne hôtelière de San Francisco spécialisée dans les hôtels-boutiques.
LE « PETIT PLUS »	Saint-Trop sur des skis.

Mountains and Movies...
Sundance, Sundance

Sundance, Sundance

Utah **337**

Mountains and Movies

Some of the best getaway havens owe their existence to the extraordinary vision of a single person. Thoreau's Walden Pond is famous because of the poet's need to experience solitude and harmony with nature. If Thoreau had been rich and had cared to share his solitude with the public, he might have come up with Sundance, the arts community and resort nestled in the Utah mountains. Sundance is the creation of Robert Redford, the movie star and director who soared to fame in the 1970s in the movie about the American outlaws, Butch Cassidy and the Sundance Kid. Redford, a bit of an outlaw himself, turned his back on the chic Hollywood scene and used his earnings to buy nearly 25,000 acres of virgin land in the Utah foothills for a family hideaway. But by the 1980s, his idea of a private retreat had evolved into something else – an arts community, built in total harmony with the environment (no structures rise above the tree line). At Sundance, cottages are made of natural materials, wood and stone, and decorated in Native American motifs. The buildings fade into the exhilarating landscape; at Sundance the land is the star. You can ski here, of course, and hike and do all the mountain resort things; but you can also make pottery, go to concerts, watch the latest independent films, and, in the spa, enjoy an organic footbath while surrounded by the music of Navajo Indians. "Creativity is at the core of Sundance culture," says Redford of his one-man's-dream retreat. "It is our contribution to a better world."

Books to pack: "The Outlaw Trail: A History of Butch Cassidy and his Wild Bunch" by Charles Kelly.

The true story of the famous American outlaw will immerse you in the culture of the old Utah West.

Sundance
8841 N. Alpine Loop Road
Sundance, UT 84604
USA
Tel. +1 801 225 4107
Fax +1 801 226 1937
Email: concier@sundance-utah.com
Website: www.sundanceresort.com
www.great-escapes-hotels.com

DIRECTIONS	Located about 50 miles (80 km) southeast of Salt Lake City airport.
RATES	$$$
ROOMS	95 guest cottages and twelve rental houses.
FOOD	Restaurants include the Tree Room (gourmet dinners), the Foundry Grill (casual Western cooking) and the Owl Bar, a restored 1890s interior moved here from Wyoming.
HISTORY	Originally the family retreat of film star cum environmentalist Robert Redford; the resort opened in 1988.
X-FACTOR	Culture, art, and cutting edge cinema, plus stunning snowcapped mountains.

Berge und Filme

Manche der schönsten Paradiese auf Erden haben ihre
Existenz einem Visionär zu verdanken. »Walden Pond«, ein
Naturschutzgebiet in Massachusetts, ist das Werk des Dich-
ters und Pazifisten Henry D. Thoreau, der sich im 19. Jahrhundert von der Zivilisation zurückzog, um in Einklang mit
der Natur zu leben. Eine ähnliche Entstehungsgeschichte
hat Sundance in Utah. Der Künstler- und Ferienort wurde
vom Filmstar und Regisseur Robert Redford gegründet.
Redford hatte den Ort 1969 während der Dreharbeiten zu
»Butch Cassidy und Sundance Kid« entdeckt. Der Film, der
ihn zum Star machte, handelte von zwei Western-Banditen.
Und genauso wenig wie sich die Filmhelden ans Gesetz hiel-
ten, beugte sich Redford den Regeln Hollywoods. Er kehrte
der Filmstadt den Rücken und kaufte in den Bergen von
Utah gut 10.000 Hektar unberührtes Land. Dort plante er
eine Ferienresidenz für sich und seine Familie. In den
Achtzigern entwickelte sich aus dem privaten Rückzugsort
ein ökologisches Künstler-Resort. Kein Gebäude ist höher als
die Bäume, die Cottages mit Indianer-Motiven sind aus
Naturmaterialien wie Holz und Stein. Das Resort fügt sich
in die traumhafte Landschaft ein und überlässt den großen
Auftritt der Natur. Selbstverständlich kann man hier Ski lau-
fen und wandern, wie es sich für einen richtigen Bergort
gehört. Man kann aber auch töpfern, Konzerte besuchen,
den neuesten Independent-Film anschauen, sich im Spa mit
einem biologischen Fußbad verwöhnen lassen und dazu
Navajo-Musik lauschen.

Buchtipp: »The Outlaw Trail: A History of Butch Cassidy and his Wild Bunch« von Charles Kelly.

Die wahre Geschichte eines berühmt-berüchtigten Banditen
vor dem Hintergrund der amerikanischen Western-Kultur.

Les sommets du cinéma

Certains des meilleurs refuges doivent leur existence à la
vision extraordinaire d'un seul homme. La cabane de
Thoreau à « Walden Pond » est née de son besoin de solitude
et d'harmonie avec la nature. S'il avait été riche et avait sou-
haité partager sa solitude avec le public, ce grand poète
aurait peut-être choisi « Sundance », une communauté
d'artistes nichée dans les montagnes de l'Utah. « Sundance »
est l'œuvre de Robert Redford, star et réalisateur de cinéma,
qui a accédé à la célébrité dans les années soixante-dix grâce
à un film sur les hors-la-loi américains « Butch Cassidy et
Sundance Kid ». Redford, un peu hors-la-loi lui-même, a
tourné le dos au glamour hollywoodien et cassé sa tirelire
pour acheter 10 000 hectares de terres vierges au pied des
montagnes de l'Utah et s'y réfugier avec sa famille.
Toutefois, dès les années quatre-vingt, son concept d'un
refuge familial avait évolué en une communauté d'artistes,
construite en complète harmonie avec l'environnement
(aucun bâtiment ne dépasse la cime des arbres). Toutes les
maisons sont construites avec des matériaux naturels, de la
pierre et du bois, et ornées de motifs indiens. Elles se fon-
dent dans un paysage revigorant. À « Sundance », la star,
c'est la nature. Naturellement, on peut y skier, faire des randonnées et tout ce qu'on fait dans une station de montagne.
Mais on peut également pratiquer la poterie, aller au concert, voir les derniers films indépendants, et, dans le spa,
goûter à un bain de pied organique en écoutant de la musique navajo. « La créativité est au cœur de la culture de
Sundance », déclare Redford de sa retraite de rêve. « C'est
notre contribution à un monde meilleur ».

Livres à emporter : « Les mémoires de Butch Cassidy » de Martin Roger.

L'histoire vraie du célèbre hors-la-loi racontée par un auteur
de polars.

ANREISE	Rund 80 km südöstlich vom Flughafen Salt Lake City.
PREISE	$$$
ZIMMER	95 Gäste-Cottages und zwölf Häuser.
KÜCHE	Der »Tree Room« mit Gourmetmenüs im Kerzenlicht und der »Foundry Grill« mit Spezialitäten aus dem amerikani-schen Westen. Die »Owl Bar« stammt aus den 1890ern und wurde von Wyoming nach Sundance transportiert.
GESCHICHTE	Ursprünglich die Ferienresidenz von Filmstar und Umweltschützer Robert Redford; seit 1988 ein Resort.
X-FAKTOR	Kultur, Kunst und angesagtes Kino; atemberaubend schö-ne Berglandschaft.

ACCÈS	À 80 km au sud-est de l'aéroport de Salt Lake City.
PRIX	$$$
CHAMBRES	95 chalets et douze maisons à louer.
RESTAURATION	Le « Tree Room » (cuisine gastronomique dans un cadre romantique), et le « Foundry Grill » (cuisine sim-ple de l'Ouest américain); on peut prendre un verre au « Owl Bar », dont la décoration datant des années 1890 a été restaurée et apportée du Wyoming.
HISTOIRE	Initialement retraite familiale de l'acteur écologiste Robert Redford, la station a ouvert ses portes en 1988.
LE « PETIT PLUS »	Culture, art et cinéma d'avant-garde.

Wild West, High Style...
Amangani, Jackson Hole

Amangani, Jackson Hole

Wild West, High Style

In the 19th century, the high wide valley of Jackson Hole, Wyoming probably boasted more bison and elk than people. Fur trappers and Native Americans passed through this remote area with its thrilling view of the snowcapped and jagged Grand Teton Mountains, the youngest range in the Rockies. Today's Jackson Hole is a world away from those old Wild West days – the hunters and trappers are history now, replaced by well-heeled skiers who rub elbows with celebs and other assorted Hollywood royalty.

Still, the Amangani resort retains, in its design and ambience, something of the spirit of those old frontier days. Like all the outposts of the famous Aman chain, it incorporates the culture of its place. The Amangani structure doesn't rise up to disturb the view of the mountains and big sky; instead, the three story building is cut into the hillside, and clings to the contours of the East Gros Ventre Butte, melding with the landscape. Western materials are used throughout – from the Oklahoma sandstone of its exterior, to the Pacific redwood furniture and sconces, the woven cowhide and faux-wolf fur chairs in the suites. Call it Western minimalist. It's an Aman, so of course there's a good spa, but more energetic guests may want to head to the Amangani's library, with its collection of Native American and Western literature, and borrow a book. Take it with you to the outdoor heated infinity pool, and read of bygone days surrounded by a stunning view of the mountains and valleys where the buffalo once roamed.

Books to pack: "The Big Sky" and "The Way West" by Alfred B. Guthrie.

Epic adventure stories of America's vast frontierlands.

Amangani	
1535 North East Butte Road	
Jackson Hole, WY 83001	
USA	
Tel. +1 307 734 7333	
Fax +1 307 734 7332	
Email: amangani@amanresorts.com	
Website: www.amanresorts.com	
www.great-escapes-hotels.com	

DIRECTIONS	Located near Jackson Hole, Wyoming, about 25 miles (40 km) from Jackson Hole airport.
RATES	$$$$
ROOMS	40 suites, including 29 suites, six deluxe suites, four Amangani suites and the Grand Teton suite.
FOOD	Breakfast, lunch and dinner at The Grill, a 65-seat dining room.
HISTORY	Opened in 1998.
X-FACTOR	Admire the Grand Tetons from the heated 113 foot (35 metre) long infinity pool.

Der Wilde Westen ganz komfortabel

Im 19. Jahrhundert gab es im weiten Hochtal von Jackson Hole in Wyoming wahrscheinlich mehr Bisons und Elche als Menschen. Einzig Pelzjäger und Indianer durchquerten die gottverlassene, wunderschöne Gegend der Grand Teton Mountains, die jüngste Bergkette der Rockies. Jäger und Trapper gibt es hier nicht mehr – der Wilde Westen ist längst Vergangenheit. Ersetzt wurden sie durch eine gutbetuchte Schickeria, die hier gemeinsam mit bekannten Persönlichkeiten und Hollywood-Stars ihren Skiurlaub genießt. Das Amangani-Resort hat etwas vom Geist des Wilden Westens in die heutige Zeit hinübergerettet. Wie in allen Resorts der Aman-Gruppe wird das lokale kulturelle Erbe gehegt und gepflegt. Die Anlage kuschelt sich sanft in die Landschaft ein, die Konturen des dreistöckigen Gebäudes führen entlang der Kuppe des »East Gros Ventre« und lassen den Blick auf die Berge und den weiten Himmel frei. Auch in der Materialwahl bleibt das Resort lokal verwurzelt: Von den Außenwänden aus Sandstein aus Oklahoma über Möbel und Wandleuchter aus Pazifik-Rotholz bis hin zu den mit Kuhfell- oder falschem Wolfspelz bezogenen Stühlen in den Suiten – alles ist typisch für den Westen. Am treffendsten kann man die Ausstattung wohl mit Western-Minimalimus bezeichnen. Zu den Annehmlichkeiten des Resorts gehört selbstverständlich auch ein Top-Spa. Wer sich nicht nur vom Wohlfühl-Programm einlullen lassen will, findet in der Bibliothek eine interessante Auswahl an Indianer- und Wild-West-Literatur. Besonders gut in den alten Zeiten schwelgen lässt sich am geheizten Outdoor-Infinity-Pool. Von dort kann man ab und zu den Blick über die atemberaubend schönen Berge und Täler schweifen lassen.

Buchtipps: »Der weite Himmel« und »Der Weg nach Westen« von Alfred B. Guthrie.
Epische Abenteuergeschichte mit Fortsetzung aus dem Wilden Westen.

Le Far West, version luxe

Au 19e siècle, la grande vallée de Jackson Hole, dans le Wyoming, comptait sans doute plus de bisons et d'élans que d'habitants humains. Seuls les trappeurs et les Indiens traversaient cette région isolée dominée par les sommets déchiquetés et perpétuellement enneigés du Grand Téton, la plus jeune chaîne de montagnes des Rocheuses. Aujourd'hui, Jackson Hole est bien loin des mystères de l'Ouest, les chasseurs et trappeurs ont cédé la place aux skieurs rupins qui côtoient les célébrités et autres sommités du gratin hollywoodien.

Néanmoins, l'Amangani conserve, par son décor et son atmosphère, quelque chose de l'esprit de la conquête de l'Ouest. Comme toutes les antennes de la célèbre chaîne hôtelière Aman, il intègre la culture du lieu. Le bâtiment ne dépasse pas trois étages pour ne pas déranger la vue sur les montagnes et l'immensité du ciel. Il semble taillé dans le flanc rocheux et s'accrocher à la crête de l'« East Gros Ventre » Butte, se fondant dans le paysage. Partout, on a utilisé des matériaux de l'Ouest américain : grès de l'Oklahoma à l'extérieur ; meubles et appliques en séquoia du Pacifique à l'intérieur ; cuirs de vache tressés et fauteuils tapissés en faux loup dans les suites. On peut parler de minimalisme western. Comme dans tous les hôtels Aman, le spa est à la hauteur de la situation mais les plus énergiques préféreront peut-être passer par la bibliothèque, choisir un livre dans sa collection d'ouvrages sur les Indiens et le Far West, et l'emporter dans la piscine chauffée à ciel ouvert pour se plonger dans les récits du bon vieux temps devant un panorama époustouflant de pics et de vallées où paissaient autrefois les bisons.

Livre à emporter : « Oregon-Express » de Alfred B. Guthrie.
Aventures épiques dans le Grand Ouest au 19e siècle, suite de « The Big Sky »

ANREISE	Rund 40 km vom Flughafen in Jackson Hole, Wyoming.
PREISE	$$$$
ZIMMER	40 Suiten, davon 29 Suiten, sechs Deluxe-Suiten, vier Amangani-Suiten und die Grand-Teton-Suite.
KÜCHE	Frühstück, Mittag- und Abendessen im »The Grill« mit 65 Sitzplätzen.
GESCHICHTE	1998 eröffnet.
X-FAKTOR	Bad im geheizten Infinity-Pool mit Blick auf den Grand Teton.

ACCÈS	Situé près de Jackson Hole, dans le Wyoming, à environ 40 km de l'aéroport de Jackson Hole.
PRIX	$$$$
CHAMBRES	40 suites, réparties en 29 suites simples, six suites de luxe, quatre suites Amangani et la suite Grand Téton.
RESTAURATION	Petit-déjeuner, déjeuner et dîner servis au « Grill », une salle à manger de 65 couverts.
HISTOIRE	Ouvert en 1998.
LE « PETIT PLUS »	Admirer le Grand Téton depuis la piscine de trente-cinq mètres de long, chauffée et en plein air.

> **citysearch.com**
Citysearch is the most urban-wise online guide to shopping, eating, and exploring more than 100 of America's major cities. The articles are written by local writers, who provide very opinionated and independent reviews of everything from spas to hotels to takeout food. The website is fairly easy to use, and well organized by category and location.

> **concierge.com**
This is the website of Condé Nast Traveller, one of the top travel magazines in the U.S. Most of the destination content comes from their extensive archive of magazine articles. Since the magazine's target audience is the upscale, sophisticated traveler, this is the place to find out where the hot new hotels and restaurants are. It also has links to airline and hotel booking sites.

> **fivestaralliance.com**
This is a booking service for luxury hotels worldwide, but their North American section is comprehensive, and lists 481 properties. There are nice descriptions and pictures of each hotel – if money is no object, this is the hotel website to check first.

> **fodors.com**
The website of the American guidebook company wins the prize as the best travel guide for U.S. and Canadian destinations. They usually won't give you the trendiest and most cutting edge travel information, but Fodor's is a safe and reliable bet for the essential info on American places large and small. Best of all, the site mixes the guidebook information with new reports from the field, especially written for the website, so it is very up to date.

> **greatcanadiantravel.com**
This Winnipeg-based travel agency organizes active and adventure tours worldwide, but their specialty is Canada – they offer hiking expeditions in the Canadian Rockies, camping trips to British Colombia, and they can arrange travel to the remote and difficult-to-reach Canadian Arctic.

> **historichotels.org**
This is the website of the National Historic Trust Hotels of America. It functions as both a guide and a booking service for 218 hotels in the 50 states that, according to the American National Preservation Society, have maintained their historic architecture and ambience.

> **hoteldiscounts.com**
This is the number one American site for booking hotels at a discount. It offers probably the largest selection of U.S. hotels online, usually at far cheaper rates than the published ones. But make sure you choose carefully, since this website features hotels of all types and comfort ranges, and the hotel descriptions aren't always thorough!

> **citysearch.com**
Der beste Online-Stadtführer der USA mit Shopping-Adressen, Restaurants, Hotels und Tipps in 100 amerikanischen Städten. Unabhängige lokale Journalisten berichten aus ihrer Stadt über neue Spas, interessante Hotels und gutes Essen. Die Website ist sehr einfach zu navigieren und übersichtlich in Kategorien und nach Lage eingeteilt.

> **concierge.com**
Das Magazin »Condé Nast Traveller« gehört zu den führenden Reisemagazinen der USA. Die Website des Magazins informiert umfassend über verschiedene Destinationen, zum größten Teil aus dem Archiv des Printtitels. »Condé Nast Traveller« hat die Nase stets zuvorderst und weiß über die neuesten und angesagtesten Restaurants und Hotels Bescheid. Mit Links zu Airline- und Hotel-Booking-Sites.

> **fivestaralliance.com**
Ein übersichtlicher Booking-Service für Luxus-Hotels auf der ganzen Welt, davon 481 in Nordamerika. Jedes Hotel wird mit ansprechenden Fotos und informativen Texten vorgestellt. Für Leute, bei denen Geld keine Rolle spielt.

> **fodors.com**
Fodor's ist einer der bekanntesten Reiseführer in Amerika. Die Online-Version mit Reisezielen in den USA und Kanada wurde sogar ausgezeichnet. Trendige Adressen sucht man in diesem seriösen und zuverlässigen Führer vergeblich, doch nach der Lektüre von Fodor's weiß man über alles Wichtige Bescheid. Die Website wird laufend aktualisiert und ist immer auf dem neuesten Stand.

> **greatcanadiantravel.com**
Dieses Reisebüro aus Winnipeg organisiert Aktiv- und Abenteuerreisen auf der ganzen Welt, hat sich aber auf Kanada spezialisiert. Im Angebot stehen Wander-Expeditionen in den kanadischen Rocky Mountains, Zeltausflüge nach British Columbia und Reisen in die schwer zugängliche kanadische Arktis.

> **historichotels.com**
Die Website der »National Historic Trust Hotels of America« ist Reiseführer und Booking-Service in einem. Die 218 Hotels in 50 Staaten wurden von der »National Preservation Society« nach historisch und architektonisch relevanten Kriterien ausgewählt.

> **hoteldiscounts.com**
Hotelbuchungen zu Discountpreisen und die wahrscheinlich größte Online-Auswahl an Hotels in den USA. Die Online-Preise sind meist ein gutes Stück tiefer als die offiziellen. Doch aufgepasst: Die Beschreibungen der Hotels sind nicht immer ganz treffend. Infos prüfen!

> **citysearch.com**
Citysearch est le plus dégourdi et urbain des guides pour faire son shopping, bien manger et explorer plus d'une centaine de grandes villes des États-Unis. Les articles sont rédigés par des auteurs locaux qui offrent des vues très personnelles et indépendantes sur tous les aspects qui nous intéressent, des spas aux hôtels en passant par les traiteurs. Le site web est assez facile à naviguer et bien organisé par catégories et lieux.

> **concierge.com**
Page web de Condé Nast Traveller, un des premiers magazines de voyages aux États-Unis. La plupart des informations sont puisées dans leurs immenses archives. Le magazine ciblant une clientèle aisée et sophistiquée, c'est là que vous trouverez les nouveaux hôtels et restaurants branchés. Propose également des liens vers des sites de réservation de billets d'avion et d'hôtels.

> **fivestaralliance.com**
Service de réservation pour des hôtels de luxe dans le monde entier. Sa rubrique « Amérique du nord » est très complète, citant 481 adresses. Chaque hôtel est présenté avec de belles descriptions et photos. Si les prix ne vous rebutent pas, c'est le site d'hôtels à examiner en premier.

> **fodors.com**
La page web de la maison d'édition américaine de guides de voyages remporte la palme du meilleur guide pour les destinations aux États-Unis et au Canada. Il ne vous donnera peut-être pas les données les plus branchées et pointues mais il est très fiable pour les informations essentielles sur les sites petits et grands des U.S. et du Canada. En outre, il mêle les informations issues de ses guides à des comptes rendus sur le terrain, rédigés spécialement pour le site, si bien qu'il est très à jour.

> **greatcanadiantravel.com**
Cette agence de voyage basée à Winnipeg organise un tourisme actif et d'aventures dans le monde entier mais sa spécialité est le Canada. Elle propose des randonnées dans les Rocheuses canadiennes et des séjours en camping en Colombie Britannique. Elle peut aussi organiser des voyages dans les régions reculées et difficiles d'accès de l'Arctique canadien.

> **historichotels.org**
Site web du National Historic Trust Hotels of America. Il sert à la fois de guide et de service de réservation pour 218 hôtels dans les 50 états qui, selon l'Association des parcs nationaux américains, ont conservé leur architecture et leur atmosphère historique.

> **hoteldiscounts.com**
C'est le site américain le plus populaire pour réserver une chambre à prix discount. Il offre probablement la plus vaste sélection d'hôtels aux États-Unis, généralement à des tarifs nettement inférieurs à ceux annoncés officiellement. Mais veillez à bien choisir car il présente des hôtels de toutes gammes et niveaux de confort et ses descriptions ne sont pas toujours complètes !

TASCHEN Web Picks: click here for even more places to escape to: Of course there are thousands of travel sites to virtual-visit on the Internet, these are some of our favourites - but

> **hotspringsenthusiast.com**
> If you are a hot springs lover, this is a site you'll want to bookmark: A guide to hot springs and geothermal spots in the United States, with links to local information on specific hot springs, geographical coordinates of their locations, and some rather technical information on the water, its temperature and composition.

> **hotwire.com**
> A travel discount website where you can pick up excellent last minute deals on U.S. hotels (although to get the best deals, you may have to book "blindfolded", without seeing the name of the hotel, only the price, the number of stars and the location). One of the best features of the website is that it offers great prices on rental cars, an essential element of most U.S. vacations.

> **literarytraveler.com**
> If you are a literature buff who wants to travel in the footsteps of your favorite author, Literarytraveler.com is the place to go. Here you'll find travel articles to help you plan your literary pilgrimages. While the site has an international focus, it is particularly strong on American writers like John Steinbeck, Jack Kerouac and Henry David Thoreau. There are also some regional guides that will help you explore the locations made famous by the writers of the American West and South.

> **mapquest.com**
> Mapquest is an invaluable interactive map tool to help you figure out where you are and where you are going in the U.S. Just plug in the address of your location and destination, and it will provide you with step by step driving directions.

> **motelamericana.com**
> A lovingly compiled website and homage to America's classic 1950s era motels. Organized state by state, with terrific photographs of the hotels, their neon signs, and vintage postcards. They also have small articles on the history of various vintage motels, and a section where they keep track of which motels are opening, closing, or being renovated.

> **mtsobek.com**
> Mountain Travel Sobek is a high-end, well-known San Francisco based travel company specializing in small-group adventure and outdoors tours. They offer trips worldwide, but have an especially good selection of treks to remote backcountry areas of the U.S. and Canada.

> **ngtraveler.com/traveler/**
> The website of National Geographic Traveler magazine, one of the best sources for informative writing about places in America. The magazine's motto is "all travel, all the time", and its articles capture the atmosphere and culture of places, while also providing solid logistical how-to information.

> **hotspringsenthusiast.com**
> Für Fans heißer Quellbäder. Die Site listet alle heißen Quellen und geothermischen Orte der USA zusammen mit entsprechenden Links auf. Informationen über Lage, Wasserqualität, Temperaturen etc.

> **hotwire.com**
> Last-Minute-Angebote von Hotels in den USA zu Discountpreisen. Damit erhält man zwar den besten Deal, kauft aber die Katze im Sack. Zunächst wird nur Preis, Kategorie und Standort des Hotels bekanntgegeben – der Name erst nach der Buchung. Super Angebote für Mietwagen – bei USA-Reisen ein wichtiger Punkt.

> **literarytraveler.com**
> Auf den Spuren großer Autoren: Die Website publiziert Reiseberichte über Orte, die von berühmten Schriftstellern ins Rampenlicht gerückt wurden. Wie Kuba von Ernest Hemingway und Prag von Franz Kafka. Die Website ist international ausgerichtet, setzt den Fokus aber auf amerikanische Autoren wie John Steinbeck, Jack Kerouac und Henry David Thoreau. Literary Traveler organisiert auch verschiedene Literatur-Reisen.

> **mapquest.com**
> Die Online-Stadtpläne sind eine super Orientierungshilfe. Schritt-für-Schritt-Wegbeschreibungen erhält man, indem man ganz einfach Start- und Zieladresse eingibt.

> **motelamericana.com**
> Alles über die typisch amerikanischen Motels der Fünfziger. Nach Staaten gegliedert. Liebevoll gestaltet mit tollen Bildern von Motels, Neonbeschriftungen und Vintage-Postkarten. Historische Hintergründe und Informationen zu Eröffnungen, Schließungen und Umbauten.

> **mtsobek.com**
> Die Reiseagentur »Mountain Travel Sobek« in San Francisco spezialisiert sich auf Abenteuerreisen und Outdoor-Touren in kleinen Gruppen auf der ganzen Welt. Besonders interessant ist die Auswahl an Treks in den Naturgebieten der USA und Kanada.

> **ngtraveler.com/traveler/**
> Die Website des Magazins »National Geographic Traveler« gehört zu den am besten recherchierten Quellen zu Reisezielen in Amerika. Die Berichte liefern nicht nur verlässliche Basisinformationen, sondern fangen auch Atmosphäre und Kultur ein.

> **hotspringsenthusiast.com**
> Si vous aimez les sources chaudes, c'est un site à classer parmi vos favoris. Ce guide des sources chaudes et géothermales des États-Unis comporte des liens vers des informations locales sur les lieux spécifiques, leurs coordonnées géographiques et des données plutôt techniques sur la qualité de l'eau, sa température et sa composition.

> **hotwire.com**
> Un site de voyages à prix réduits où vous pouvez faire d'excellentes affaires de dernière minute sur les chambres d'hôtels américains (mais, pour les meilleures occasions, il vous faudra peut-être réserver à l'aveuglette, sans connaître le nom de l'hôtel, uniquement ses tarifs, le nombre d'étoiles et l'emplacement). Cerise sur le gâteau: il offre d'excellents prix sur la location de voitures, élément essentiel pour la plupart des vacances aux États-Unis.

> **literarytraveler.com**
> Pour les amateurs de littérature qui souhaitent marcher sur les traces de leur auteur favori, Literarytraveler.com est le site rêvé. Vous y trouverez des articles pour vous aider à préparer votre pèlerinage littéraire. Le site a vocation internationale mais est particulièrement riche en ce qui concerne des écrivains américains tels que John Steinbeck, Jack Kerouac et Henry David Thoreau. Certains guides régionaux vous aideront également à explorer les lieux rendus célèbres par les romanciers du Grand Ouest et du Sud.

> **mapquest.com**
> Mapquest est un outil cartographique interactif des plus précieux qui vous aide à repérer où vous êtes et où vous allez aux États-Unis. Tapez l'adresse de votre emplacement et de votre destination et il vous fournira les indications routières étape par étape.

> **motelamericana.com**
> Un site web et un hommage amoureusement composé sur les motels américains des années cinquante. Organisé par états, avec de superbes photos des motels, de leurs néons et des cartes postales d'époque. Comporte également des articles sur l'histoire de différents établissements et une rubrique citant ceux qui ouvrent, ferment ou sont en rénovation.

> **mtsobek.com**
> Mountain Travel Sobek une célèbre agence de voyage haut de gamme basée à San Francisco spécialisée dans le tourisme d'aventure en petits groupes et les séjours en plein air. Elle propose des voyages dans le monde entier mais dispose d'une très bonne sélection de randonnées dans des recoins sauvages des États-Unis et du Canada.

> **ngtraveler.com/traveler/**
> Site web du magazine National Geographic Traveler, une des meilleures sources d'articles instructifs sur différents sites des États-Unis. La devise de la revue est «tous les voyages, tout le temps». Ses articles capturent l'atmosphère et la culture des lieux tout en procurant des informations logistiques fiables et solides.

be warned, you can spend hours roaming the web finding great places to get away to; it's very addictive. Just add www. to these addresses, and bon voyage!

› **nps.gov**
The U.S. national park service's official website is the place to go if you are planning to spend time exploring America's natural treasures. It is the most comprehensive guide to all of the National Parks, historic sites, monuments and memorials in the United States.

› **quikbook.com**
A very good website for finding discounted prices on rooms in mid- to upper-priced boutique and design hotels. On the Quikbook website you will find a small and exclusive selection of stylish hotels in major American cities, usually priced at $20 to $50 below the rack rate. The site is nicely designed and easy to use, and the format makes it easy to compare the amenities at the different hotels.

› **randmcnally.com**
A comprehensive website for U.S. maps from America's leading mapmaker, this is a good place to go to plot your course – or just to daydream about your road trip across the United States.

› **roadfood.com**
This website is a terrific guide to the best small restaurants, barbeque joints and diners to be found along America's backroads. Where do you get the best hot dogs, ribs, or apple pie in America? This site will give you the answer – it is like a Michelin Guide to American regional homecooking.

› **roadsideamerica.com**
A quirky, funny and useful guide to the most offbeat and kitschy alternative tourist attractions, museums and events in the U.S.

› **roadsidepeek.com**
A fun website that chronicles the fast-disappearing American roadside architecture of the 50s, 60s and 70s, mostly in photos. There are sections on "Tiki", on neon signs, "space station" styled gas stations and classic American diners. An entire section is devoted to the architecture along the fabled highway, Route 66.

› **seeamerica.org**
It is a great place to begin research for a trip, because it is filled with detailed and practical background and logistical information on each of the 50 states. The website also has a calendar of special events and festivals in the U.S. The site's most useful feature is its direct links to each state's official tourism website.

› **tablethotels.com**
This hotel search engine and booking service specializes in "unique hotels for global nomads" – in other words, design-conscious, stylish retreats. The website's design is as stylish as its subject, and it has lots of good photographs to help you select your hotel.

› **nps.gov**
Die offizielle Website des »National Park Service« informiert über die Nationalparks der Vereinigten Staaten. Leicht verständlicher Führer mit Informationen zu historischen Sehenswürdigkeiten, Naturwundern und Denkmälern.

› **quikbook.com**
Eine kleine, exklusive Auswahl schicker Hotels in allen größeren US-Städten zu Discountpreisen. Pro Buchung liegt ein Preisnachlass zwischen umgerechnet 15 € und 40 € drin. Die ansprechende Website ist einfach zu navigieren und clever aufgebaut, sodass man die Hotels direkt miteinander vergleichen kann.

› **randmcnally.com**
Auf der Website von Amerikas führendem Kartografen kann man eine virtuelle Reise durch Amerika unternehmen. Ideal für die Planung einer richtigen Reise oder auch einfach nur zum Träumen.

› **roadfood.com**
Amerikas Straßen führen zum Teil durch weites, spärlich besiedeltes Land ohne städtisches Restaurantangebot. Dieser Essführer sagt, wo man auf der Fahrt quer durch Amerika die besten Hot Dogs, Ribs oder den besten Apfelstrudel findet. So etwas wie ein Michelin-Guide für amerikanische Hausmannsküche.

› **roadsideamerica.com**
Witzige Website mit Touristenattraktionen, Museen und Veranstaltungen außerhalb des Mainstreams.

› **roadsidepeek.com**
Eine Hymne auf die vom Aussterben bedrohte amerikanische Roadside-Architektur der fünfziger, sechziger und siebziger Jahre. Besonders interessant: die Kapitel zu »Tiki«-Stil, kunstvollen Neonschriften, Vintage-Tankstellen und -Diners und der legendären »Route 66«.

› **seeamerica.org**
Detaillierte und praktische Hintergrundinformationen über die 50 Staaten der USA mit einem Kalender zu Veranstaltungen und Festivals. Links zu den Tourismusbüros der einzelnen Staaten.

› **tablethotels.com**
Buchungssystem für angesagte und stylische Hotels auf der ganzen Welt. Das Design der Website ist ganau so schick wie die darin aufgeführten Hotels. Mit tollen Fotos.

› **nps.gov**
Le site officiel du département américain des parcs nationaux est incontournable si vous projetez d'aller explorer les trésors naturels américains. C'est le guide le plus complet sur les parcs nationaux, les lieux historiques, les monuments et les sites commémoratifs des États-Unis.

› **quikbook.com**
Un excellent site web pour trouver des tarifs réduits sur les chambres dans les hôtels boutiques et design de la gamme moyenne à supérieure. Vous y trouverez une petite sélection d'hôtels de charme dans les principales villes des États-Unis, généralement environ 15 à 40 € moins cher que le prix officiel. Le site est joliment conçu et facile à naviguer ; et son format permet de comparer aisément les services et agréments des différents établissements.

› **randmcnally.com**
Un site de cartes américaines complet édité par le plus grand cartographe des États-Unis. C'est le lieu idéal pour préparer son itinéraire, ou simplement rêver de voyager sur les routes à travers l'Amérique.

› **roadfood.com**
Ce site est un guide formidable des meilleurs petits restaurants, troquets à barbecue et « diners » situés sur les sentiers battus. Où trouver le meilleur hot-dog, les meilleures côtelettes ou la meilleure tarte aux pommes ? Il connaît la réponse. C'est le guide Michelin de la cuisine régionale et familiale des États-Unis.

› **roadsideamerica.com**
Un guide décalé, drôle et utile des attractions touristiques, musées et manifestations les plus excentriques et kitsch des États-Unis.

› **roadsidepeek.com**
Un site sympa qui documente l'architecture routière américaine des années cinquante, soixante et soixante-dix, en voie d'extinction rapide, principalement en photos. Il y a des rubriques sur « Tiki », les enseignes au néon, les pompes à essence style « station spatiale » et les « diners » classiques américains. Toute une partie est consacrée à l'architecture le long de la légendaire « Route 66 ».

› **seeamerica.org**
Un lieu parfait pour commencer ses recherches avant de planifier un voyage, car il est rempli d'informations détaillées et pratiques tant culturelles que logistiques sur chacun des 50 états. Son atout le plus utile : ses liens directs avec les sites des offices du tourisme officiels de chaque état.

› **tablethotels.com**
Ce moteur de recherche et centre de réservation d'hôtels est spécialisé dans les « hôtels uniques pour nomades planétaires », à savoir des établissements chic et design. La conception du site est aussi élégante sur son sujet, et il comporte de nombreuses bonnes photos pour vous aider dans votre choix.

TASCHEN Web Picks:
Eine Reise nach Nordamerika zu planen macht meist genauso viel Spaß wie die Reise selbst. Das Abenteuer beginnt bereits im Internet auf den verschiedenen Reise-Webseiten mit vielen nützlichen und stets aktuellen Informationen. Dabei findet man ein schickes Hotel, ein günstiges Mietauto oder auch ein vegetarisches Restaurant im Landesinneren, dort wo sonst nur Viehherden weiden. Auf anderen Webseiten gibt es außergewöhnliche Sehenswürdigkeiten zu entdecken, die sonst in keinem Reiseführer zu finden sind. Viel Spaß bei Ihrer Internet-Surf-Tour durch Amerika und gute Reise!

Les bons tuyaux de TASCHEN:
Préparer une escapade en Amérique du Nord peut être aussi palpitant que le voyage lui-même. Avec ces sites web de voyage, vous vous croirez déjà sur la route, vivant la grande aventure américaine. Vous y trouverez des informations pratiques régulièrement remises à jour qui vous aideront à réserver un joli hôtel, à louer une voiture à un bon prix et même à trouver un restaurant végétarien en plein coeur du pays du bétail. D'autres sites vous indiqueront des attractions culturelles situées hors des sentiers battus et qui ne figurent dans aucun guide. Surfez bien et bon voyage!

› **travelcanada.ca**
The official website of the Canadian Tourism Commission is a well-designed introduction to Canada and its attractions. Has separate sections for each Canadian province, and nice photography.

› **vegetarianusa.com**
The no-frills design of this website will give you a headache, but it is a fountain of useful information if you are interested in natural lifestyles (or if you have been traveling on American highways too long and are sick of eating McDonald's). There are lists of health food stores and restaurants in each of the 50 states, and there is also a very useful listing (with links) of spiritual centers, yoga spas and retreats nationwide.

› **vrbo.com/vacation-rentals/usa**
VRBO stands for "vacation rentals by owner". It is a fascinating website filled with thousands of cottages, apartments and houses put up for rental by their owners (usually by the week or month). Most of the ads have pictures, and the places range from palatial to cozy and everything in between. Besides being a great armchair travel pastime (you can "shop" for American real estate, or just peep into other people's vacation houses), this is a very useful website if you are planning a trip to a remote location where there are few hotels – for instance, the smaller Hawaiian islands.

› **woodalls.com**
For campers, this is a practical website that has everything you need to know to plan a RV trailer or tent camping trip in the U.S. Even if you would never dream of spending two weeks in a trailer, the site provides an entertaining glimpse into that culture, a style of travel popular with millions of Americans.

› **worldhum.com**
Worldhum is the best U.S.-based travel writing website; it features essays and articles, mostly by American writers. But its most useful feature for the American traveler is that it includes a digest of the most interesting travel articles in U.S. newspapers. The digest is updated weekly, so this is a good place to check for the latest news and trends in American travel. It also has a good section of travel web links.

› **zagats.com**
Zagats guide is the bible of U.S. gourmets; the company surveys restaurant-goers and then compiles their comments into restaurant reviews. The online guide is an interactive engine that can point you to restaurants around the U.S. by cuisine, price, popularity and location. It is an invaluable tool for dining in the U.S., which is probably why you have to buy a subscription to use this site.

› **travelcanada.ca**
Offizielle Website der »Canadian Tourism Commission«. Übersichtliche Informationen über Kanada und seine Sehenswürdigkeiten. Jede Provinz hat ein eigenes Kapitel.

› **vegetarianusa.com**
Das Design der Website mag handgestrickt daherkommen, doch wer Wert auf gesunde Ernährung legt, ist hier richtig. Gerade in den USA mit den vielen Fast-Food-Ketten ist eine solche Quelle äußerst wertvoll. Die Site listet Naturkost-Märkte, Bioläden und vegetarische Restaurants nach Staaten auf. Mit Links zu spirituellen Zentren, Yoga-Studios und -Retreats.

› **vbro.com/vacation-rentals/usa**
VBRO steht für »Vacation Rentals by Owner«. Die Website listet Tausende von Apartments, Häuser und Cottages, die von ihren Besitzern zur Miete (üblicherweise pro Woche oder Monat) ausgeschrieben werden. Das Angebot reicht von palazzoartigen Häusern bis zu einfachen Apartments - und alles dazwischen. Fotos geben einen Eindruck vom Mietobjekt. Ideal für Reisende, die nicht in einem Hotel übernachten wollen oder keines finden, wie z.B. auf abgelegenen Inseln Hawaiis.

› **woodalls.com**
Nützliche Informationen für Camper, die einen Trip mit dem Wohnmobil oder Zelt durch die USA planen. Auch interessant als Feldstudie über die Reise-Kultur und den Lifestyle von Millionen von Amerikanern.

› **worldhum.com**
Essays und Berichte über Destinationen in Amerika und weltweit. Dazu eine interessante Auswahl an Reiseberichten, die in amerikanischen Zeitungen veröffentlicht wurden. Die Website wird wöchentlich aktualisiert und gibt Auskunft über aktuelle Reise-Trends. Gute Auswahl an Reise-Links.

› **zagats.com**
Die Bibel jedes amerikanischen Gourmets. Zagat publiziert Restaurantbewertungen, die aufgrund von Befragungen bei Restaurantbesuchern verfasst werden. Die Online-Version ist interaktiv; so kann man die Restaurants nach verschiedenen Kriterien wie Küche, Preis, Beliebtheit und Lage suchen. Nur im Abonnement zu haben; doch wer in den USA gut essen will, kommt kaum um diese Investition herum.

› **travelcanada.ca**
Le site officiel de la Canadian Tourism Commission constitue une introduction bien conçue au Canada et à ses attractions. Possède des sections séparées pour chaque province et de belles images.

› **vegetarianusa.com**
Le design sans chichi de ce site web vous donnera la migraine mais c'est une mine d'informations utiles si vous vous intéressez aux styles de vie proches de la nature (ou si vous voyagez sur les routes des Etats-Unis depuis trop longtemps et n'en pouvez plus des MacDo). Il propose une liste de boutiques et de restaurants bios dans chacun des cinquante états, ainsi qu'un inventaire très utile (avec les liens) des centres de ressourcement spirituels, des spas de yoga et des retraites dans tout le pays.

› **vrbo.com/vacation-rentals/usa**
VRBO signifie « vacation rentals by owner ». Ce site fascinant est rempli de milliers de cottages, d'appartements et de maisons, proposés à la location par leurs propriétaires (généralement à la semaine ou au mois). La plupart des annonces sont accompagnées de photos et les lieux vont du palais au nid douillet, avec tout ce qui peut y avoir entre les deux. On peut le consulter en rêvassant dans son fauteuil, chercher de bons plans immobiliers, ou simplement reluquer l'intérieur des résidences secondaires des autres. Le site est particulièrement utile si vous projetez un séjour dans un lieu isolé où il y a peu d'hôtels, comme les plus petites îles d'Hawaï.

› **woodalls.com**
Pour les campeurs, ce site pratique possède tout ce que vous avez besoin de savoir pour préparer un voyage en caravane ou sous la tente aux États-Unis. Même si vous préféreriez vous casser un bras plutôt que de passer deux semaines dans une caravane, il offre un aperçu divertissant de cette culture, une façon de voyager appréciée par des millions d'Américains.

› **worldhum.com**
Worldhum est le meilleur site web américain sur la littérature de voyage, présentant des essais et des articles signés d'auteurs principalement américains. Mais, pour le voyageur, c'est donc un site à consulter son condensé des articles les plus intéressants parus dans la presse américaine. Mis à jour chaque semaine, c'est donc un bon site à consulter pour les dernières nouvelles et tendances du tourisme aux États-Unis. Il possède également une bonne rubrique de liens vers d'autres sites de voyage.

› **zagats.com**
Le guide Zagat est la bible des gourmets américains. La compagnie interroge les amateurs de bonnes tables puis compile leurs commentaires sous forme de critiques. Le guide en ligne est un moteur interactif qui vous oriente vers les restaurants en fonction de la cuisine, des prix, de la fréquentation et de l'emplacement. C'est un outil très précieux pour bien manger aux États-Unis, ce qui explique sans doute pourquoi l'abonnement au site est payant.

© 2009 TASCHEN GmbH
Hohenzollernring 53, D-50672 Köln
www.taschen.com

ORIGINAL EDITION:	© 2006 TASCHEN GmbH
EDITOR AND LAYOUT:	Angelika Taschen, Berlin
PROJECT MANAGER:	Stephanie Bischoff, Cologne
EDITORIAL COORDINATION:	Julia Krumhauer, Cologne
LITHOGRAPH MANAGER:	Thomas Grell, Cologne
FRENCH TRANSLATION:	Philippe Safavi, Paris
GERMAN TRANSLATION:	Simone Ott Caduff, California
DESIGN:	Lambert und Lambert, Düsseldorf

PRINTED IN	China
ISBN	978-3-8365-1485-9

To stay informed about upcoming TASCHEN titles, please request our magazine at www.taschen.com/magazine or write to TASCHEN, Hohenzollernring 53, D-50672 Cologne, Germany; contact@taschen.com; Fax: +49-221-254919. We will be happy to send you a free copy of our magazine, which is filled with information about all of our books.